CEASE TO CONTEND

HEALING A NATION THROUGH CHRISTLIKE CIVILITY IN POLITICS

CEASE TO CONTEND

HEALING A NATION THROUGH
CHRISTLIKE CIVILITY IN POLITICS

RODNEY B. DIESER PH.D., LMHC
FOREWORD BY THOMAS B. GRIFFITH

CFI
An imprint of Cedar Fort, Inc.
Springville, Utah

© 2025 Rodney B. Dieser, Ph.D.
All rights reserved.

No part of this book may be reproduced in any form whatsoever, whether by graphic, visual, electronic, film, microfilm, tape recording, or any other means, without prior written permission of the publisher, except in the case of brief passages embodied in critical reviews and articles.

This material is neither made, provided, approved, nor endorsed by Intellectual Reserve, Inc. or The Church of Jesus Christ of Latter-day Saints. Any content or opinions expressed, implied or included in or with the material are solely those of the owner and not those of Intellectual Reserve, Inc. or The Church of Jesus Christ of Latter-day Saints." Permission for the use of sources, graphics, and photos is also solely the responsibility of the author.

Paperback ISBN 13: 978-1-4621-4922-3
eBook ISBN 13: 978-1-4621-4923-0

Published by CFI, an imprint of Cedar Fort, Inc.
2373 W. 700 S., Suite 100, Springville, UT 84663
Distributed by Cedar Fort, Inc., www.cedarfort.com

Library of Congress Control Number: 2025931924

Cover design by Shawnda Craig
Cover design © 2025 Cedar Fort, Inc.
Edited and Typeset by Liz Kazandzhy

Printed in the United States of America

10 9 8 7 6 5 4 3 2 1

Printed on acid-free paper

To Louie, a devoted friend.

Contents

Foreword..1

1 George Washington's Farewell Address,
  Doctrine and Covenants 136:23, and Pahoran.............3

2 Listening to People with Different Political
  Views: Reframing Your Mindset.........................23

3 Listening to Understand Instead of Listening to Argue......57

4 Media Literacy to Become Informed in Politics............81

5 Richard Haass's Ten Habits of Good Citizens............115

6 Five Cases of Exemplary Leaders Who Ceased to Contend..125

About the Author...135

Foreword

By Judge Thomas B. Griffith[1]

LATTER-DAY SAINTS HAVE A SENSE THAT WE HAVE A STEWARDSHIP TO protect the Constitution of the United States and the principles upon which it is based. We also have a sense that we need to be vigilant and watchful because those principles are in constant need of support. They are fragile possibilities in the best of times, and this is not the best of times. Social scientists tell us that our nation has never been so polarized since the Civil War tore asunder the "bonds of affection" that helped create our union. Contempt has replaced reasoned argument, and enmity is the fuel that fires much of our politics.

How are we to "support and defend" the Constitution in these new and troubling circumstances? What can each of us do? Learning the history of the Constitution, the meaning of its provisions, and the structure of the government it creates is a good start, but that is not enough. In early July 1787, the delegates to the Constitutional

---

1. Thomas B. Griffith was appointed to the United States Court of Appeals for the DC Circuit by President George W. Bush in 2005. In 2021, President Joe Biden appointed him to the Presidential Commission on the Supreme Court. See https://hls.harvard.edu/faculty/thomas-griffith/ for more information. Judge Griffith is a member of The Church of Jesus Christ of Latter-day Saints.

Convention in Philadelphia faced the real prospect of failure, yet by mid-September they had produced the Constitution. This surprising turn of events has been called the "Miracle at Philadelphia." And yet there was nothing mysterious about how the delegates succeeded in overcoming vast political and regional divides to create the Constitution. In his letter transmitting the Constitution to Congress, George Washington explained that the Constitution was "the result of a spirit of amity and of that mutual deference and concession which the peculiarity of our political circumstances rendered indispensable."[2] Amity. Mutual deference. Concession. It was the exercise of these virtues that created the Constitution. To preserve the Constitution today requires the exercise of the same virtues.

But how do we create "a spirit of amity"? How do we practice "mutual deference"? What does "concession" mean? Rodney Dieser is uniquely qualified to help us understand how to develop and put into practice these necessary virtues so that we can better carry out our responsibility to "support and defend" the Constitution. He is an active member of The Church of Jesus Christ of Latter-day Saints, and his professional training in human behavior—which includes working as a licensed mental health counselor and as a researcher who has published over one hundred academic articles and seven books related to human behavior—makes him qualified in providing faith-based action steps to help the reader learn how to listen to understand others. His thesis is authentic and pragmatic: Once we understand others, we can seek to modify and to unify. He is a committed and believing Latter-day Saint who in this timely book puts to use his professional training to help us understand how to carry out the charge President Oaks has given to Latter-day Saints during this time of toxic political polarization: "On contested issues, we should seek to moderate and to unify."[3]

---

2. "Letter of the President of the Federal Convention, Dated September 17, 1787, to the President of Congress, Transmitting the Constitution," Yale Law School, accessed Jan. 17, 2025, https://avalon.law.yale.edu/18th_century/translet.asp.

3. Dallin H. Oaks, "Defending Our Divinely Inspired Constitution," *Ensign* or *Liahona*, May 2021, 105–108.

1

George Washington's Farewell Address, Doctrine and Covenants 136:23, and Pahoran

As members of The Church of Jesus Christ of Latter-day Saints, we are encouraged to engage in the political process in an informed and civil manner, respecting that fellow members of the Church come from various backgrounds and experiences and have differences of opinion in partisan political matters. We are also encouraged to be responsible, and part of that obligation is to become knowledgeable and well-versed about social, civic, and political issues and events. This is clearly and explicitly outlined in the "Political Neutrality and Participation" statement by The Church of Jesus Christ of Latter-day Saints, which was updated on June 1, 2023.[4] A humble aim of this small book is to aid in this process during an era of so much political deception, distortions, half-truths, and intense political division and polarization.

---

4. "Political Neutrality and Participation," The Church of Jesus Christ of Latter-day Saints, June 1, 2023, https://newsroom.churchofjesuschrist.org/official-statement/political-neutrality.

Cease to Contend draws from three historical events: (1) President Washington's farewell address, (2) Doctrine and Covenants 136:23, and (3) Pahoran's example in the Book of Mormon. It outlines a three-step process to increase civility in social and political thought and engagement. *Cease to Contend* is additionally rooted in Aristotle's introspection, modern-day social science, and principles from The Church of Jesus Christ of Latter-day Saints.

To a lesser degree, this book also draws from one of Socrates' most famous sayings, "To know thyself is the beginning of wisdom."[5] Socrates believed self-knowledge could be developed through conversation, such as listening to others with different views. He also believed that busyness distracted people from essential questions about themselves and that quiet reflection was needed. Chapter 2, which is focused on identifying within ourselves six prevalent cognitive distortions couched specifically in political thinking, is based on the axiom "To know thyself is the beginning of wisdom." One of the reframing techniques you will learn about in chapter 2 is Socratic questioning, obviously named after Socrates.[6]

George Washington's Farewell Address and Doctrine and Covenants 136:23

Washington's farewell address was published on September 19, 1796, as a written letter to "friends and fellow-citizens" printed in *Claypoole's American Daily Advertiser*, an American newspaper headquartered in Philadelphia. The address was circulated approximately ten weeks before the presidential electors cast their votes in the 1796 election and, by design, hit newspapers as Washington rolled out of

---

5. The words "know thyself" were inscribed on the Temple of Apollo at Delphi in ancient Greece. While many believe that Socrates invented it, this phrase has been attributed to many ancient Greek thinkers.

6. One good source to better understand Socrates (and stoicism) and apply his thinking to modern-day psychology is the book *The Stoicism Workbook: How the Wisdom of Socrates Can Help You Build Resilience and Overcome Anything Life Throws at You* (2024), written by Waltman, Codd, and Pierce. These authors also outline the strong relationships between cognitive distortion, cognitive behavioral therapy, and the ideas of Socrates.

Philadelphia in his coach to return to his beloved Mount Vernon. Washington did not want to interfere in the upcoming election.[7]

The farewell address is considered long, at 7,641 words, and Washington sought out Alexander Hamilton during the writing process. It covers many things, such as a warning that national identity must trump local attachments, as Washington feared that hyperpartisanship and polarization could destroy our nation. What is most relevant to *Cease to Contend* is that Washington challenged people to improve their performance as citizens. He urged citizens to engage in responsible civic behavior, which included being responsible in the political process and informed about social and political issues. In Washington's second term as president, there was intense division and polarization (between federalists and anti-federalists), and various newspapers were printing stories that were heinously untrue about George Washington, such as he was secretly trying to create an American monarchy and taking bribes from the British kingdom.

Doctrine and Covenants 136:23 is a revelation that was given to Brigham Young on January 14, 1847.[8] As president of the Quorum of the Twelve at the death of Joseph Smith, Brigham Young was responsible for leading the Saints westward toward the Rocky Mountains. Autumn of 1846 found 15,000 exiled Latter-day Saints temporarily living at Winter Quarters near Omaha, Nebraska, and Council Bluffs, Iowa. Their prophet, Joseph Smith, had been killed, along with his brother Hyrum, while being held in Carthage Jail. The Saints were driven from the city of Nauvoo and were walking to present-day Utah. Among the Saints was contention and wild bickering, and

---

7. The information in this section regarding George Washington's farewell address is taken from Ron Chernow, *Washington: A Life* (Penguin Books, 2011), 752–63. For a primary source, Washington's farewell address can be read online, with annotated notes, at the Library of Congress; see https://www.loc.gov/resource/mgw2.024/?sp=229&st=text.

8. The information regarding Doctrine and Covenants 136 is from Chad M. Orton, "This Shall Be Our Covenant," in *Revelations in Context: The Stories Behind the Sections of the Doctrine and Covenants*, ed. Matthew S. McBride and James Goldberg (Intellectual Reserve, Inc., 2016), 307–314. See also https://www.churchofjesuschrist.org/study/manual/revelations-in-context/this-shall-be-our-covenant.

members of the Church needed to "cease to contend with one another." Contention is a heated disagreement, and this revelation ended such contention and brought calmness and unity.

Becoming Better Citizens and Ceasing to Contend is Needed Today

This same counsel—to become responsible and informed about social and political issues and to cease to contend with others—is greatly needed today considering the highly conflict-driven political climate in the United States where heated disagreement is everywhere, from local venues like community libraries and public schools all the way to state and federal elections.

In the last five years, unprecedented contention has been linked to the federal election. Two examples are the assassination attempt on Donald Trump on July 13, 2024, as he was campaigning near Butler, Pennsylvania, and the January 6 (2021) United States Capitol attack in which a mob attempted a coup two months after Trump's defeat in the 2020 presidential election. There are more examples of extraordinary disputations in politics. For example:

- On January 6, 2021, another mob gathered at the home of former Georgia election worker Ruby Freeman, accusing her of helping to steal the 2020 election and referring to her as a "professional vote scammer." Freeman reported that the FBI warned her that she should flee for her safety.[9]
- Georgia's Republican secretary of state Brad Raffensperger, his wife, Tricia, and their family received threats of violence months after the 2020 election, also subject to false claims of being complicit in votes being stolen away from Donald Trump.[10]

---

9. Andrew Goudsward, "Georgia Election Worker 'Terrorized' by Threats After 2020 Election," *Reuters*, Dec. 13, 2023, https://www.reuters.com/world/us/georgia-election-worker-terrorized-by-threats-after-2020-election-2023-12-13/.

10. Linda So, "Special Report: Trump-Inspired Death Threats Are Terrorizing Election Workers," *Reuters*, June 11, 2021, https://www.reuters.com/article/world/us-politics/special-report-trump-inspired-death-threats-are-terrorizing-election-workers-idUSKCN2DN14L/.

- In September 2024, a second assassination attempt on Donald Trump happened while he was playing golf in West Palm Beach, Florida.[11]
- On Thanksgiving Day in 2024, five of Connecticut's Congress members were notified of bomb threats targeting their homes.[12]
- In 2022, the husband of former House Speaker Nancy Pelosi was violently attacked at his home in San Francisco based on the assailant's belief in conspiracy theories.[13]
- In 2017, an attacker, who openly expressed hatred toward Republicans, opened gunfire during a baseball practice of Republican lawmakers who were preparing for the congressional baseball game. Representative Steve Scalise was critically injured.[14]

In 2024, Cynthia Miller-Idriss, director of research at American University's "Polarization & Extremism Research & Innovation Lab," clearly articulated that polarizing rhetoric that captures political opponents as existential threats is a problem at both the elite level and

---

11. "Ryan Wesley Routh Indicted for Attempted Assassination of Former President Trump," United States Department of Justice, Sept. 24, 2024, https://www.justice.gov/opa/pr/ryan-wesley-routh-indicted-attempted-assassination-former-president-trump.
12. Megan Lebowitz and Alex Seitz-Wald, "Connecticut Congress Members Targeted with Bomb Threats on Thanksgiving," *NBC News*, Nov. 28, 2024, https://www.nbcnews.com/politics/congress/connecticuts-democratic-congress-members-targeted-bomb-threats-thanksg-rcna182156.
13. Olga R. Rodriguez, "The Man Accused of Attacking Nancy Pelosi's Husband Was Caught up in Conspiracies, Defense Says," *Associated Press,* Nov. 9, 2023, https://apnews.com/article/nancy-pelosi-husband-attacked-trial-28f189e4b005b8f7d413df0b79f2aeaa.
14. Pete Williams, Alex Moe, and Erik Ortiz, "Congressman Steve Scalise, Three Others Shot at Alexandria, Virginia, Baseball Field," *NBC News,* June 14, 2017, https://www.nbcnews.com/news/us-news/congressman-steve-scalise-shot-alexandria-virginia-park-n772111.

among ordinary people in everyday life.[15] As George Washington stated just under 230 years ago, Americans need to become better citizens so they contend less.

Counsel from Latter-day Saint Leaders and Sources on Contention

If you go to the website of The Church of Jesus Christ of Latter-day Saints and look up the word *contention*, it states, "Contention brings unhappiness into our homes and into our lives. Satan is the father of contention and all the misery that it brings. Our Father in Heaven wants us to fill our lives with love and eliminate contention."[16] It then lists these scriptural references:

- 3 Nephi 11:29–30: "For verily, verily I say unto you, he that hath the spirit of contention is not of me, but is of the devil, who is the father of contention, and he stirreth up the hearts of men to contend with anger, one with another."
- Doctrine and Covenants 136:23: "Cease to contend one with another; cease to speak evil one of another."
- Mosiah 4:14–15: "And ye will not suffer your children that they go hungry, or naked; neither will ye suffer that they transgress the laws of God, and fight and quarrel one with another, and serve the devil, who is the master of sin, or who is the evil spirit which hath been spoken of by our fathers, he being an enemy to all righteousness. But ye will teach them to walk in the ways of truth and soberness; ye will teach them to love one another, and to serve one another."
- Proverbs 13:10: "Only by pride cometh contention."
- Matthew 5:25: "Agree with thine adversary quickly"

---

15. "Why Political Violence and Violent Threats Are on the Rise in the United States," Public Broadcast Services, July 14, 2024, https://www.pbs.org/newshour/show/why-political-violence-and-violent-threats-are-on-the-rise-in-the-united-states.
16. "Contention," *Family Home Evening Resource Book* (1997), https://www.churchofjesuschrist.org/study/manual/family-home-evening-resource-book/lesson-ideas/contention.

In 2024, President Dallin H. Oaks shared the following about contention:

> Another of our Savior's teachings seems to require reemphasis in the circumstances of our day.
>
> This is a time of many harsh and hurtful words in public communications and sometimes even in our families. Sharp differences on issues of public policy often result in actions of hostility—even hatred—in public and personal relationships. This atmosphere of enmity sometimes even paralyzes capacities for lawmaking on matters of importance where most citizens see an urgent need for some action in the public interest.
>
> What should followers of Christ teach and do in this time of toxic communications? What were His teachings and examples?
>
> It is significant that among the first principles Jesus taught when He appeared to the Nephites was to *avoid contention*. While He taught this in the context of disputes over religious doctrine, the reasons He gave clearly apply to communications and relationships in politics, public policy, and family relationships. Jesus taught:
>
> *"He that hath the spirit of contention is not of me, but is of the devil, who is the father of contention, and he stirreth up the hearts of men to contend with anger, one with another.*
>
> "Behold, this is not my doctrine, to stir up the hearts of men with anger, one against another; but this is my doctrine, that such things should be done away."
>
> In His remaining ministry among the Nephites, Jesus taught other commandments closely related to His prohibition of contention. We know from the Bible that He had previously taught each of these in His great Sermon on the Mount, usually in precisely the same language He later used with the Nephites.[17]

Likewise, President Russell M. Nelson has counseled, "Contention drives away the Spirit—every time. Contention reinforces the false notion that confrontation is the way to resolve differences; but it never is. Contention is a choice. Peacemaking is a choice. You have your agency to choose contention or reconciliation. I urge you to choose to be a peacemaker, now and always."[18]

---

17. Dallin H. Oaks, "Following Christ," *Liahona*, Nov. 2024, 25; emphasis added.
18. Russell M. Nelson, "Peacemakers Needed," *Liahona*, May 2023, 100.

As members of the Church, we also can heed George Washington's call to become better citizens, and more importantly, we can follow the scriptures and modern-day Church leaders to cease to contend.

Political and Social Contention Among the Saints in the Last Five Years

As members of The Church of Jesus Christ of Latter-day Saints, we are not perfect, and it is easy to move toward contention, especially when it comes to political and social issues. I witnessed unfathomable contention among members of my church family after Iowa governor Kim Reynolds issued mask mandates in November 2020 due to the COVID-19 pandemic. Hal Boyd's 2021 article in the *Deseret News*, titled "'Let's Go Brandon' Chants Don't Belong at BYU Games," underscored a crude and mocking gesture that Brigham Young University (BYU) fans directed toward the president of the United States. ("Let's Go Brandon" is a political catchphrase and internet meme used as a euphemism for an unbelievable, shocking, and distasteful commentary that is related to swear words directed toward President Joe Biden.) Boyd outlined, "Such demonstrations fall beneath the mark of good citizenship, let alone the more lofty aims of Christian discipleship which call on us to love our enemies."[19]

I might be wrong, but I would venture to guess that many BYU fans did not know what the term meant and just joined in to jeer President Joe Biden, and some may have just started chanting to be part of the cheering, not knowing what the term meant. But it is still troubling to hear throngs of BYU fans, most of whom are members of the Church, intoning such a repulsive phrase. Boyd referenced the comments of President Dallin H. Oaks, sharing his concern with how Americans and Church members are handling the national issues that divide us and his call for a better way forward by reconciling adverse

---

19. Hal Boyd, "'Let's Go Brandon' Chants Don't Belong at BYU Games," *Deseret News*, Nov. 16, 2021, https://www.deseret.com/opinion/2021/11/16/22785863/lets-go-brandon-chants-dont-belong-at-byu-games-football-gop-nascar-joe-biden-cougars-brigham-young/. Hal Boyd, who served as past editor of the *Deseret News*, currently serves as executive editor of *Deseret Magazine* and chief of staff to the president of Brigham Young University.

positions through respectful negotiation. As reported in the *Deseret News*, a 2024 poll underscored that more than 43 percent of Utahns believe that violence against the government can be justified (in this poll, 46 percent of Utah Republicans stated it could be justified, compared to 38 percent of Democrats). Among members of the Church, this survey identified that 35 percent reported that violence against the government can be justified, while 65 percent believe it can never be justified.[20] Contention precedes violence.

As Judge Thomas B. Griffith commented in the foreword of this book, "Contempt has replaced reasoned argument, and enmity is the fuel that fires much of our politics." Healthy political disagreement is the foundation of democracy. Democracy cannot exist without opposing views, public policies, or an oppositional party. However, people can disagree politically in respectful ways and without contention.

As further evidence of the state of political contention that our country is in, a 2021 Pew Research study indicated that 59 percent of Americans find political conversations with those they disagree with as "stressful and frustrating," up 9 percent since 2019. More specifically, 58 percent of Republicans and Republican-leaning independents say they find talking politics with people they disagree with stressful, up 11 percentage points since 2019, and 60 percent of Democrats and Democrat-leaning independents say they find such conversations taxing and frustrating, up 7 percent since 2019. Interestingly, this study also found that nearly two-thirds of white adults (65 percent) say they find talking about politics with people they disagree with to be stressful—much higher than Black (43 percent), Hispanic (47 percent), and Asian (53 percent) adults.[21]

---

20. Dennis Romboy, "Is Violence Against the Government Ever Justified? 4 in 10 Utahns Say Yes," *Deseret News*, Nov 1, 2024, https://www.deseret.com/politics/2024/11/01/politicial-violence-assassination-2024-election-campaign-utah-poll/.

21. Ted Van Green, "Republicans and Democrats Alike Say It's Stressful to Talk Politics with People Who Disagree," Pew Research Center, Nov. 23, 2021, https://www.pewresearch.org/short-reads/2021/11/23/republicans-and-democrats-alike-say-its-stressful-to-talk-politics-with-people-who-disagree/.

Pahoran as an Example from the Book of Mormon

One of the most vivid examples of "ceasing to contend" with others and listening to understand comes from the exchange between Pahoran, the chief judge (governor) of Zarahemla, and Captain Moroni, a righteous Nephite military commander, in Alma 60–61 of the Book of Mormon. Moroni begins to address Pahoran "by way of condemnation" (Alma 60:2) because he believes Pahoran has betrayed him. Moroni accuses him of neglect and slothfulness and even wonders if he might be a traitor (see Alma 60:18). Pahoran is responsible for sending Captain Moroni war provisions but has been unable because there was a coup against him and he was leading a government in exile. Moroni has no idea of the social context surrounding Pahoran and asserts, "Ye know that ye do transgress the laws of God, and ye do know that ye do trample them under your feet" (Alma 60:33), and then exhorts Pahoran to repent of his mistakes! The problem, however, is that Moroni was mistaken, and Pahoran was actually doing his best to support Moroni.

Pahoran's example is paramount to this book, as he is well-mannered and civil in the face of Moroni's undeserved criticism and continues to hear Moroni's voice. Pahoran could have responded in many ways, including with bitterness or even contempt; however, he instead states, "In your epistle you have censured me, but it mattereth not; I am not angry, but do rejoice in the greatness of your heart" (Alma 61:9). Pahoran chooses to focus his mind on rejoicing in the greatness of Moroni's heart and not on self-talk that ruminates on being mistreated or on the poor dispositional or character traits of Moroni. Pahoran then goes even further and offers a dignified reinterpretation or reframing of Moroni's letter: "I was somewhat worried concerning what we should do. . . . But ye have said, except they repent the Lord hath commanded you that ye should go against them" (Alma 61:19–20).

In modern-day psychology, specifically in areas such as cognitive behavioral therapy, logotherapy, and positive psychology, what Pahoran did was to frame or structure his thoughts within a positive framework and not follow dysfunctional or damaging thoughts that could lead to a host of negative feelings and behaviors. As a licensed mental health counselor, I have written many treatment goals like this: "Within six weeks, the client will learn to reframe negative and fear-based thoughts to reality-based positive thinking." How we think of others, such as those we disagree with politically, has a lot to do with how we feel and behave when engaging with them or trying to hear their voice (or cancel them out and silence them). This book aims to help you, the reader, change how you think about political leaders and neighbors who think so very differently. After reading this book, I hope you, the reader, can listen to understand and not listen to argue and seek to unify. That is, I hope we can all be more like Pahoran.

In many states right now, especially in Iowa (where I live), there are political debates regarding whether teachers should be armed in schools or if schools should be places that allow no guns. The thinking of arming teachers is that it provides a quick defense system if a person walks into a school and starts shooting at children and staff. The thinking of keeping schools gun-free is that more weapons in schools will lead to more guns falling into the wrong hands, making schools less safe. I have witnessed people on both sides of this issue scream at each other in public settings. If each side thinks of the other as idiotic, deranged, stupid, rednecks / clueless liberals, and so forth, those negative thoughts will result in negative feelings and behaviors. But if a person can pause, hear another person, and then reflect—listening to understand (instead of contending)—they might realize that both sides have a principal commonality: They both want (or are united) to protect their kids because they both love their children at intense levels. Both are on the same page regarding higher-order thinking; they just disagree on the means to the end.

If we start by finding reality-based positive thoughts and common ground—and parents on both sides of this issue wanting to protect their children seem reality-based to me, firmly on common ground—it is easier to hear the other voice and then engage in the more difficult task of agreeing on something in the middle. As Stephen R. Covey stated years ago, "Seek first to understand before being understood."[22]

---

22. Stephen R. Covey, *Seven Habits of Highly Effective People* (Free Press, 1989), 235–60.

Captain Moroni is a hero to many members of the Church, and for obvious reasons. But I find it remarkable that in Alma 60–61, we learn that a very righteous man can make honest mistakes. While serving as a bishop in Cedar Falls, Iowa, I worked hard to be righteous and repented daily, but I still made honest mistakes. Moroni's mistake was making a judgment without understanding the social context, and it is something I have also done. I am sure you, the reader, have done this too! Following automatic (first) thoughts and not questioning them is at the core of cognitive distortions—which are exaggerated or irrational thought patterns involved in the onset or perpetuation of negativity and sometimes psychopathological states, such as depression and anxiety—and working on these cognitive distortions is the heart and soul of cognitive behavioral therapy. This book teaches how to identify six prevalent cognitive distortions couched specifically in political thinking and how to reframe them so we can listen to understand. Instead of following automatic thoughts of seeing the other as an enemy, we start by pausing such thoughts and listening to another person so we can understand them. That is how we begin to modify and unify. It starts with an individual mindset.

In a recent *Deseret News* article, Thomas B. Griffith, writing about the early Constitution, outlined that the framers tried to understand one another and were willing to give up some things they valued dearly for the sake of unity.[23] Akhil Amar, one of our era's most significant Constitutional scholars, has outlined how George Washington had the cognitive aptitude to find a middle ground when engaging with anti-federalists.[24] Judge Griffith posited how vital President Oaks' general conference talk was in directing Saints to seek to moderate and unify contested political issues.[25] In modern-day psychology, this is known as cognitive agility (also known as cognitive flexibility or

---

23. Thomas B. Griffith, "Latter-Day Saints Have a Distinct Charge to Uphold the Constitution," *Deseret News*, Aug. 31, 2023, https://www.deseret.com/opinion/2023/8/31/23854125/defend-us-constitution-latter-day-saints.

24. Akhil Reed Amar, *The Words That Made Us: America's Constitutional Conversations, 1760–1840* (Basic Books, 2021), 275–326.

25. Dallin H. Oaks, "Defending Our Divinely Inspired Constitution," *Ensign* or *Liahona*, May 2021, 105–108.

elasticity), the ability to consider different perspectives and opinions and find a middle ground. It is also known as being open-minded and is at the center of good mental health.[26] The opposite, cognitive rigidity, is the inability to adapt or change mentally and is at the root of many mental health issues, relationship problems, interpersonal and community conflict, and hatred.[27]

A Three-Step Approach to Decrease Contention and Increase Social and Political Civility

Cease to Contend presents a three-step approach to increase social and political civility and is broken into six chapters. Although there are wise sociological and ecological methods[28] that can be taken to lower social and political strife and increase community and partisan politeness and respect, this book takes a personal approach that each individual can make behavioral changes to decrease contention. The three behavioral changes are:

1. Identify your cognitive distortions to increase social and political civility and lower contention.
2. Develop better listening skills so you can listen to people who have different political views.
3. Improve media literacy skills so you can better navigate through social and mass media.

---

26. Gabriella Rosen Kellerman and Martin E. P. Seligman, *Tomorrowmind: Thriving at Work with Resilience, Creativity, and Connection—Now and in an Uncertain Future* (Simon Element, 2023), 174–78.
27. Although there are scores of studies that demonstrate how cognitive rigidity is at the root of many mental health disorders, one recent study that uses neuroscientific evidence to show this is Giommi et al., "The (In)flexible Self: Psychopathology, Mindfulness, and Neuroscience," *International Journal of Clinical and Health Psychology* 24, no. 4 (2023): article 100381, https://doi.10.1016/j.ijchp.2023.100381.
28. Jonathan Haidt suggests the following structure changes: change the ways that primary elections are run, electoral districts are drawn, and how candidates raise money for their campaigns. See Jonathan Haidt, *The Righteous Mind: Why Good People Are Divided by Politics and Religion* (Vintage, 2012), chap. 12.

There is an abundance of research that demonstrates that one of the best approaches to lower civic disagreement is positive contact and interpersonal relationships with people who think differently. Haidt captures this well, stating, "If you really want to open your mind, open your heart first. If you can have at least one friendly interaction with a member of the 'other' group, you'll find it far easier to listen to what they're saying, and maybe even see a controversial issue in a new light."[29] But I would argue it takes a little homework to increase the probability of having a friendly interaction with people who think differently from you politically and socially, and that homework is the three steps outlined in this book.

Chapter Overviews

Drawing on forty years of research in cognitive behavioral therapy, chapter 2 will focus on cognitive distortions. That is, step one is for readers to learn how to identify these cognitive distortions in themselves (not in others) and how to reframe them so they can listen to understand people who have different political views and ideas.

One of the most common cognitive distortions is extreme black-and-white thinking. In political dialogue, it comes out as "my side is right and yours is wrong," Such thinking creates a superior dichotomy of them and us, with little thought of a middle ground. Sometimes negative labels can be added to this cognitive distortion, such as "What a complete idiot—they're so stupid and so wrong. How can they be that dumb?" Such thoughts lead to negative feelings and behaviors toward "the other." But if a person can reframe such automatic thoughts—to something like "It's not that one person is right and the other wrong; we've had very diverse life experiences, and they think about the issue differently"—they will feel less negativity toward others who think differently. Another reframe can be "I'm overacting and need to calm down. If I listen, I might be able to understand their thinking and learn something." Another might be "Although we may have to agree to disagree, if I listen and show respect, our relationship

---

29. Jonathan Haidt, *The Righteous Mind: Why Good People Are Divided by Politics and Religion* (Vintage, 2012), 364.

might improve, and they might be willing to hear my voice." I believe all of these reframed thoughts will decrease the feelings of negativity when compared to the first cognitive distortions of "My side is right and yours is wrong" or "What a complete idiot." Hopefully, readers can learn to pause or suspend their automatic thoughts to hear another person with accuracy, demonstrating dignity toward others with whom they disagree.

Chapter 2 identifies six prevalent cognitive distortions couched specifically in political thinking as well as twelve ways a person can reframe automatic cognitive distortions into reality-based positive ways of thinking. Doing this should decrease the intense feelings of dislike, anger, and even hatred toward people who have different social and political values and ideas.

Step two is learning how to listen, and chapter 3 is focused on the science and art of listening. As you will learn from the historical scholarship presented in chapter 3 and throughout this book, both George Washington and Abraham Lincoln had an incredible ability to listen to people they disagreed with, and they were both open-minded and avid readers. Chapter 3 will teach the skill set of listening, including eight listening actions, such as summarizing, paraphrasing, and asking questions to hear another person with greater accuracy, clarity, depth, and breadth. That is, the key is learning how to listen to understand, not learning how to listen to argue or shame another person. Chapter 3 will also build on President Nelson's talk from 1991 titled "Listen to Learn."

George Washington understood that in the early days of the republic, his most overriding role was to keep the Union together by "showing skeptics and critics that their voices had indeed been heard, that the promises made in ratification conventions . . . would be redeemed, not ignored.[30] Washington had the cognitive flexibility to compromise. He (and almost all the other Philadelphia signers) had rejected George Mason's proposal to create the Bill of Rights but was then open-minded enough to reflect and change his view and agree with the anti-federalists. The psychological soul of the Constitution is compromise.

---

30. Amar, *The Words That Made Us*, 309.

Chapter 4 will introduce the third step, media literacy skills. Media literacy is the ability to analyze and evaluate media, and this chapter will have an acute focus on political discourse so that the reader can attempt to be better informed about politics and understand how media, linked to profit, attempts to dupe and hoodwink people. Media stories that are more sensational, angry, or fearful bring in more viewers, which then increases the amount of money advertising and sponsors are willing to pay. This chapter will use research-based media literacy approaches and draw on Kristoffer Boyle's article, found on the Church website, about using media literacy to find truth during an age of misinformation.[31] Chapter 4 provides five media literacy action steps that you can use to become politically knowledgeable and well-versed.

Chapter 5, the shortest chapter, will address how to be a good citizen; that is, it goes further than these three steps to provide additional suggestions toward becoming a virtuous community member. It provides an answer in the contemporary period for the axiom George Washington stated in his farewell address when he challenged all Americans to be better citizens. This chapter will draw extensively on Dr. Richard Haass's book *The Bill of Obligations: The Ten Habits of Good Citizens*, which includes lessons on how to stay open to compromise, reject violence, respect government service, and support the teaching of civics in our school systems. In many ways, this last chapter is a book review of Haass's treatise. Chapter 6 provides five cases of exemplary leaders who demonstrated cognitive elasticity, open-mindedness and ceased to contend.

Here is a summary of the steps and details that will be covered:

Step 1: Identify Your Cognitive Distortions and Reframe Them to Create a Listening Mindset

Six cognitive distortions:

1. An all-or-nothing mentality
2. Overgeneralization

---

31. Kristoffer Boyle, "Finding Truth in the Misinformation Age," *Liahona*, Oct. 2022.

3. Mental filter
4. Discounting the positives
5. Jumping to conclusions
6. Magnification and minimization

Twelve techniques to reframe cognitive distortions to decrease contention and view differing political views in a more accurate and positive way:

1. Thinking in shades of gray
2. Arguing with yourself
3. Socratic dialogue
4. Double standard technique
5. Double standard technique with a self-disclosure
6. Semantic method
7. Counting the positives
8. Inquiry
9. Examining the evidence
10. Cost-benefit analysis
11. Self-monitoring
12. Exposure or contact

STEP 2: LISTEN TO UNDERSTAND INSTEAD OF LISTENING TO ARGUE

Eight listening skills and techniques:

1. Paraphrasing
2. Clarification
3. Reflection
4. Summarization
5. Probing
6. Information-giving (listening through open-minded questioning)
7. Interpretation
8. Confrontation (or challenge)

STEP 3: DEVELOP MEDIA LITERACY TO BECOME POLITICALLY INFORMED

Five actions to improve media literacy skills:

1. Listen, without interruption, to the political candidate you oppose with respect, dignity, and an open mind (that is, hear both or multiple sides).
2. Read books written by candidates (and their core supporters) and on specific political ideas and concepts.
3. Rely on multiple and different media sources
4. Engage in less entertainment and more disciplined and somber reflection.
5. Participate in the social and political spheres in the real world.

THIS BOOK CAN HELP YOU IN OTHER AREAS OF YOUR LIFE

In one sense, the three-step approach shared in this book to increase social and political civility and decrease contention is simple. The three steps, again, are to (1) identify your cognitive distortions, (2) develop better listening skills, and (3) improve media literacy skills. In another sense, integrating these steps into everyday life will be extremely difficult. Over the years, I have worked with all sorts of people with mental health struggles, and most people change one step at a time. I would encourage readers to start with one or two steps and not try to implement the entire three-step process in one shot. Behavioral change is usually a step-by-step, continual process. Finding your cognitive distortions will be difficult, as seeing those distortions in other people is so much easier. Learning to listen to someone with very different political ideas is arduous, as it is so much easier to listen to someone who has similar political beliefs (your tribal group or social media echo chamber). Developing media literacy skills takes a significant amount of time to master. In addition, we all live busy lives.

But I believe in this three-step process; over the last twenty years, it has become habitual in my life (although I still have much to improve). I am very comfortable hearing the political views of Democrats, Republicans, Libertarians, Green Party members, and so forth. Through the various chapters, I provide examples of everyday Americans and politicians who have made such changes, and I underscore this ability in both George Washington and Abraham Lincoln, who most political scientists and historians consider to be the two best presidents in the history of our nation. I also pepper self-disclosures of how I have attempted to live these very steps in my own life. In the conclusion of this book, I share how another person, world-renowned moral and social psychologist Jonathan Haidt, has also made this change toward understanding people who think so very differently than he does about politics.

Learning this three-step approach will help you in many other areas, such as becoming a better parent, spouse, coworker, and neighbor. For example, my cognitive distortions affected my parenting and my relationship with my wife and coworkers in negative ways, and when I learned about these internal thinking errors, not only did I understand myself better (celebrating that I can become better and not beating myself up), but I could understand my wife and coworkers better. I have become a better spouse, parent, and coworker by learning how to reframe my cognitive distortions and how to listen better. And gaining better media literacy has helped me navigate media's powerful and ubiquitous influence.

I also encourage you to use prayer in implementing these three steps and use repentance and the Atonement of Jesus Christ to help change behaviors. The three steps outlined in this book are all evidence-based and research-based and are utilized in everyday mental health counseling. But using the power of Christ is most paramount, as it is the ability to draw upon the infinite power and love of Jesus Christ to overcome challenges and experience joy, peace, and consolation.[32]

---

32. Joaquin E. Costa, "The Power of Jesus Christ in Our Lives Every Day," *Liahona*, Nov. 2023, 39–41.

2

Listening to People with Different Political Views: Reframing Your Mindset

A MINDSET IS AN ATTITUDE.[33] TO LISTEN TO UNDERSTAND, ESPECIALLY with someone you disagree with, starts with your attitude. One counseling theory that helps people create different mindsets is cognitive behavioral therapy (CBT) through a process called reframing. I believe in CBT, and I use reframing daily! Reframing is the ability to identify automatic irrational thoughts—called cognitive distortions—that enter our mind and learn how to challenge, modify, or replace them.[34] I combine reframing with the power of prayer, and it helps me become a better person in numerous ways:

---

33. Carol Dweck, *Mindset: The New Psychology of Success* (Ballantine Books, 2007), 1–14. In particular, see her view of a growth mindset—a belief that our intellect and attitudes can be developed from trying new things, learning from mistakes, embracing challenges, and welcoming feedback. See also Angela Duckworth, *Grit: The Power of Passion and Perseverance* (Scribner, 2016).
34. David Burns, *Feeling Great: The Revolutionary New Treatment for Depression and Anxiety* (PESI Publishing & Media, 2020), 26–31, 182–98.

- It helps me to hear another person with greater clarity, precision, and compassion.
- It helps me have a better relationship with myself and aids emotional regulation.
- It helps me hear the Holy Ghost and, in the process, repent of my sins.
- It helps my relationships flourish, both with my wife and with my three adult sons.
- It helps me make better political decisions and actions and lowers feelings of contention with people who hold different political views.

As Latter-day Saints, we know from various Book of Mormon scriptures (for example, 2 Nephi 26:32, Mosiah 4:14, Mosiah 18:21, and 3 Nephi 11:29) that the Lord commands us not to contend with one another. Doctrine and Covenants 136:23 is so exact: "Cease to contend one with another; cease to speak evil one of another." The purpose of this book is to decrease contention in our society, allowing us to engage in the political process with respect so that democracy can flourish. Creating a positive mindset is one of the first actions you can take in listening to understand people with different political views and avoid contention.

Many treatment goals I have written as a licensed mental health counselor are based on reframing and creating a healthy mindset. Often treatment goals look like this: "In six weeks, the client's anxiety will decrease by 25 percent as measured by the Beck Anxiety Inventory by having the client reframe fear and negative thinking to reality-based positive thinking." Sometimes I write such treatment goals in the opposite direction, such as having a client increase hope or optimism by 25 percent, captured through a psychometric measurement (e.g., the Adult Hope Scale). Still, the reframing intervention remains the same, aiming to help a person change their thinking and mindset so they can then feel better and behave in a more positive way.

However, before I explain how CBT can help you identify your cognitive distortions so you can reframe them and become a better person and civil citizen, let me share a few stories of how CBT and reframing play out in my everyday life. After that, I'll share some counsel from Church leaders on the subject of reframing, followed by a brief history and overview of CBT.

How I've Used CBT in My Life

A few years ago, our youngest adult son, Zachary, who was still living with us, asked me why I always asked his two older brothers, Chayce and Jonas, what I should cook for our traditional Sunday meal and why I never asked him. I shared with Zachary that I must be doing this unconsciously (I had no awareness of this until he brought it to my attention), and my best guess is that it's probably because I only see Chayce and Jonas once a week, whereas I get to see Zachary most days. Regardless, I told him I was being thoughtless and needed to be more inclusive, and with enthusiasm, I asked, "What do you want me to cook next Sunday?" His immediate response was "Scallop pasta!"

This was a Monday, and I decided to do one better; I would surprise Zachary by making him scallop pasta on Wednesday, just for him (and Ricki, my good wife, and I). A way to communicate to Zachary that he was heard!

Because I was planning a surprise, I didn't tell him, and when he arrived home from work on Wednesday at 5 p.m., there was scallop pasta sitting on the kitchen table and a smiling father to boot! Zachary looked at me, paused in reflection, and then looked at me squarely and said, "Dad, I didn't know you were making this. I just ate a sandwich at Subway and promised Jonas and Chayce I would meet them at the gym in about thirty minutes. But I appreciate this, and I'll eat it tomorrow. Thank you!" He went to the basement, changed his clothes, and went to the gym.

I put tinfoil over his plate and placed it in the fridge, and I ate my portion an hour later when my wife came home. But something was off—I felt negative emotions. In a word, I felt annoyed. Bothered. As a CBT therapist, I have shared with hundreds of clients that when you feel negative emotions, the first step is to ask yourself, "What am I thinking right now?" So I did this and found myself thinking these sorts of automatic and irrational thoughts: "Zachary didn't appreciate my gift" and "He should have canceled with his brothers and showed his gratitude for my efforts." In CBT speak, I was engaged in two cognitive distortions—discounting the positive and blowing things out of proportion (also known as magnification or catastrophizing). I decided to talk back to my thoughts—which is a beginning step to reframing after the identification of cognitive distortions.

People *feel* and *act* what they *think*, and a cognitive distortion is a highly misleading way to think about yourself, others, the world, and political parties or individuals we disagree with or oppose.[35] Cognitive distortions are the automatic thoughts that enter our mind immediately and are irrational and off base. The key is to pause between stimulus and response, identify the automatic thoughts, and then evaluate them to see if they are irrational and not true. Sometimes our automatic thoughts are not irrational or inaccurate; sometimes they're correct (and the rest of the chapter will help you determine this, with the help of prayer and personal revelation). The most important part of talking back to irrational and misleading automatic thoughts is to be precise and reality-based/accurate. If someone was feeling negative emotions due to financial stress and reframed their thinking to "I'm going to buy a Powerball ticket and be a millionaire in a few weeks," that would not be reality-based or accurate because the percentage of winning a million-dollar jackpot is around one in twelve million.

In order to reduce or stop the negative emotion I was feeling as my mind focused on "Zachary didn't appreciate my gift," I needed to talk back to this automatic irrational negative thought. So I stated to myself, "Zachary had no idea you were doing this, and he genuinely thanked you and looked at you thoughtfully. It's great that he has a close relationship with his brothers, and rarely do those three boys have work schedules that allow them to work out together. It was just a bad break that on the evening you cooked this meal, the three Dieser boys' schedules also lined up." I then added, "This is not that big of a deal; you're blowing this out of proportion. Zachary will love this meal tomorrow, and you were thoughtful toward him. He knows that." (And Zachary did eat it the next day and loved it, thanking me a second time!)

---

35. Burns, *Feeling Great*, 15–26, 494–95.

When I focused on him looking me in the eyes and genuinely expressing gratitude, my negative emotions left me and were replaced with positive feelings. But had I kept going with my automatic thoughts—"Zachary didn't appreciate my gift" and "He should have canceled with his brothers and showed his gratitude toward my efforts"—I would have continued to feel negative emotions. Such negative emotions would then influence my behaviors, such as venting to my wife or irrationally telling Zachary he didn't appreciate my efforts, which would have spiraled into more negativity.

Negative labeling is another cognitive distortion that often enters my mind, and I have to constantly wrestle with it to reframe it. I attach a pejorative label to myself when things do not go the way I hope or envision. In political engagement, the pejorative and insulting label is directed toward the other political party or person with different political ideas and policies for social problems.

Let me tell you about my negative labeling. I have this most wonderful, four-legged friend named Louie (also known as Big Lou). I met him thirteen and a half years ago at the humane society when we adopted him. He's close to a hundred pounds, a German shepherd–Lab mix, and for over thirteen years, we have walked two to four miles every day (except when it's really hot outside). We have been on all sorts of adventures together, including being ready to fight a massive group of wild turkeys! I didn't want a dog, but Ricki talked me into it (suggesting it would be good for our sons), and the first time we met, Louie stood straight up, put his front paws on my shoulders, and looked deeply into my eyes. It was love at first sight! It was what the famous Austrian-Jewish and Israeli philosopher Martin Buber called an "I-Thou" experience.[36] Today, my sons call him "Grandpa Louis," as he is fourteen years old and the life in front of him is short.

Once or twice a month, Louie has a day when he's inside most of the time because Ricki and I can't coordinate our work schedules so that he can have a good amount of autonomy to go outside. His

---

36. An "I-Thou" experience is a holistic and genuine encounter where both parties are fully present, recognizing the inherent worth and uniqueness of the other, which causes a deep connection. See Martin Buber, *I and Thou* (Touchstone, 1971), 51–182.

backyard is perfect for him. It's a decently big yard that interfaces with the University of Northern Iowa prairie grasses with a recreation trail. You can look out for a long distance, and there is constant action for Louie to bark at—deer walk by, people walk their dogs on the trail, there are wild turkeys, and so on. Louie's German-shepherd tendency to watch and guard is on high alert, and I sense he feels a real purpose in life. After our long morning walks, Louie goes to the backyard and walks the parameters. He has dug a few large holes against the house, a cover from the snow and rain, and can see anything walking in those prairie grasses or on the recreation trail.

Until about three years ago, when Zachary moved out, Ricki was a stay-at-home mother but has since started working part-time, so Louie now has a day or two a month when he is in the house most of the day. (We let him out during lunch for fifteen minutes, not the usual hanging out in the yard for hours at a time and at his discretion). On those days, I begin with the negative labeling—I attach a pejorative label to myself—such as "I'm not a good dog owner and am ruining his life." Once in a while, I call myself a loser. My self-loathing thought patterns include that I'm not good enough and that my dog expects much better. Of course, as I focus on the negative, I experience negative emotions (e.g., sadness and feelings of worthlessness) and act irritable and grumpy. I then have to reframe, and the reframing technique I use is called "putting things into perspective." That perspective is a week-long view.

If Louie will have an inbound day on Monday, I will objectively review the rest of the week. On Tuesday and Thursday, Ricki is home all day. Wednesday and Friday, I can be home often (my university office is a five-minute drive or a twenty-minute walk) and I can complete some of my academic work in the house. Ricki and I are both home most of Saturday and Sunday. So I reframe "Louie's needs are not getting met, and I'm a loser of a dog owner" into "Louie is going to have one downer day but a wonderful six days. And even on that downer day, he gets walked twice. Rod, you are doing a pretty good job of meeting the needs of your four-legged friend." My sadness and worthlessness are transformed into feelings of cheerfulness, and my behaviors are so much more positive. My *feelings* and *behaviors* are based on what I *think*, so I feel better when I reframe the highly misleading, false, and inaccurate ways I think about myself. Later in this chapter, I'll suggest reframing or changing the highly misleading, false, and inaccurate ways we think about people and political parties that differ from or oppose our political values and beliefs.

I can tell you more stories of cognitive distortions causing alarm and anxiety, such as whenever we have a plumbing problem. My mind automatically goes to worst-case scenario thinking (known as catastrophic thinking), and I have a cognition that this is going to cost "way over $1000" when the cost is way less. Once, when I was having a drain problem, I had visualized a plumber with a jackhammer breaking up the basement floor to fix piping with a price tag in the thousands, and the only thing that happened was a plumber fixing a clog with a cost of $231. Now, when I begin thinking this way, I say to myself, "Rod, you're engaging in catastrophic thinking, and you have so much plumbing evidence to know that your automatic thoughts are not true. It will be just fine." Then calm replaces anxiety. It's common to start catastrophizing when thinking about the other political party winning an election. I have heard too many Republicans and Democrats describe that it would be "political suicide to vote for _____, and if this person wins, our nation will fall apart and spiral out of control." The following section explains how General Authorities, including prophets, have counseled us to reframe unhealthy, destructive, and sinful automatic thoughts into more Christlike thinking.

Counsel from Latter-day Saint Leaders and Sources on How to Change Our Thinking

I believe that every talk in the Sunday afternoon session of the October 2023 general conference included elements on changing our automatic thoughts to be more Christlike. President Nelson's talk, "Think Celestial," was the pinnacle. In short, our beloved prophet counseled us to reframe thoughts of life's hardships and think from a celestial perspective:

When you make choices, I invite you to take the long view—an eternal view. Put Jesus Christ first because your eternal life is dependent upon your faith in Him and in His Atonement. . . .

When you are confronted with a dilemma, think celestial! When tested by temptation, think celestial! When life or loved ones let you down, think celestial! When someone dies prematurely, think celestial. When someone lingers with a devastating illness, think celestial. When the pressures of life crowd in upon you, think celestial! As you recover from an accident or injury, as I am doing now, think celestial! . . .

As you think celestial, your heart will gradually change.[37]

Then, referencing Doctrine and Covenants 121 and 122, when Joseph Smith was praying and pleading for relief in Liberty Jail, President Nelson outlined how the Lord taught the Prophet that his horrid treatment would be for his good (reframing from the immediate horrid to the future and explaining how this experience could help a person develop and lead to an eternal reward). President Nelson stated, "The Lord was teaching Joseph to think celestial and to envision an eternal reward rather than focus on the excruciating difficulties of the day."[38] Focusing our thoughts on "What is the Lord teaching me and helping me become?" will move our behavior to communicate with God, hear His voice, feel the Spirit, and experience positive emotion. If instead our thoughts go to "God must hate me," "I must be no good and I deserve this," "There is no God and I'm all alone," or "I want to kill these people who are doing this to me," negative emotion will follow (e.g., hatred toward self, others, and even God); negative behavior will follow (e.g., distancing ourselves from Deity); and Satan will be in a better position to lead us away "carefully down to hell" (2 Nephi 28:21).

Here are two other examples of reframing from the Sunday afternoon session of the October 2023 general conference:

- Referring to 2 Kings 5:9–14 Elder Renlund shared that "when Naaman sought a cure for his leprosy, he was indignant at

---

37. Russell M. Nelson, "Think Celestial!," *Liahona*, Nov. 2023, 118.
38. Russell M. Nelson, "Think Celestial!," 118.

being asked to dip himself seven times in a nearby ordinary river. But he was persuaded to follow the prophet Elisha's counsel rather than rely on his own preconceived notions of how the miracle should occur. As a result, Naaman was healed." Naaman reframed his automatic indignant thought to one of obedience.[39]

- Elder Esplin reported the story of how during World War II, an Okinawan woman contemplated ending her life and her family's life with a hand grenade because they were in dreadful conditions, living in a cave for months and starving to death. Through a profoundly spiritual experience, she reframed her automatic thoughts and fed her family with weeds, honey from a wild beehive, and creatures caught in a nearby stream.[40]

And here are several more examples of reframing:

- Wendy Watson Nelson, the wife of President Nelson who holds a master's degree in marriage and family therapy, teaches how to reframe thoughts in her book *What Would a Holy Woman Do?*[41] She suggests a three-day experiment to go about your normal, everyday life and consistently ask yourself, "How would a holy woman [or man] do this?" This experiment teaches us to modify and reframe our thinking so that we can then change our feelings and behaviors toward being more Christlike and hearing the promptings of the Spirit better.
- The very title of one of Elder Quentin L. Cook's talks, "Live by Faith and Not by Fear," is a reframe; we replace fear thoughts with faith thoughts.[42]
- In one *Ensign* article, creatively titled "The Grapefruit Syndrome," the author writes, "As a young wife, I learned that

---

39. Dale G. Renlund, "Jesus Christ Is the Treasure," *Liahona*, Nov. 2023, 98.
40. J. Kimo Esplin, "The Savior's Healing Power upon the Isles of the Sea," *Liahona*, Nov. 2023, 108–110.
41. Wendy Nelson, *What Would a Holy Woman Do?* (Deseret Book, 2013), 1–64.
42. Quentin L. Cook, "Live by Faith and Not by Fear," *Ensign* or *Liahona*, Nov. 2007, 70–73.

the taste of marriage could be sweeter if I didn't focus on my husband's faults." What a powerful message! If you focus your mind on the positive aspects of your spouse, your marriage will be sweeter.[43]

- In a talk by Susan H. Porter directed to the Primary children, she recounts how her six-year-old granddaughter felt unimportant when she had no one to play with at the school playground. But then a reframed thought entered her mind: "Wait! I'm not alone! I have Christ!" which then caused a behavioral change to pray earnestly. The result was that a girl came to her and asked her to play. A reframed thought caused an action (prayer) that resulted in something better.[44] What I found remarkable about this talk is that President Porter is teaching a six-year-old how to reframe. She adds that the spiritual dimension, not typically found in academic and professional settings, is to build a reframe on prayer and revelation. Prayer can help a person reframe with guidance from the Holy Ghost.[45]

A Quick History of CBT: From Viktor Frankl to Aaron and Judith Beck

In addition to hearing how Church sources have encouraged reframing, I think it's also worth looking at a brief history of CBT, starting with Viktor Frankl.

---

43. Lola B. Walters, "The Grapefruit Syndrome," *Ensign*, Jan. 2011, 12.
44. Susan H. Porter, "Pray, He Is There," *Liahona*, May 2024, 77–79.
45. In regard to teaching children how to reframe to develop a healthy mindset, one of my favorite academic books is *The Optimistic Child* by Dr. Martin Seligman and colleagues from 2007 (revised edition). They present evidence-based strategies to help children reframe and prevent depression. I have used lessons in this book as a therapist and even during family home evenings when our children were young. As a mental health counselor, I have recommended Dr. Tamar Chansky's 2014 book *Freeing Your Child from Anxiety* to many parents; it demonstrates evidence-based strategies to help children with anxiety learn how to reframe automatic and irrational fear-based thoughts. The younger you can teach children how to reframe thoughts, the greater the probability of preventing mental health struggles.

I'm a student of Viktor Frankl's thinking and have read scores of his books and articles (Frankl was a prolific writer who published over 30 books and 691 articles), and I have published several articles about him. I am also a credentialed Diplomate Clinician with the American Viktor Frankl Institute of Logotherapy and accredited via the International Association of Logotherapy and Existential Analysis from the Viktor Frankl Institute in Vienna.

In 2021, Frankl's *Man's Search for Meaning*, one of life's most influential books on meaning and purpose, celebrated its seventy-fifth anniversary. Frankl's renowned Holocaust testimony has been translated into over fifty languages, sold over sixteen million copies, and is currently listed on Amazon's "Top 100 Books to Read in a Lifetime." Over the years, I have heard many Latter-day Saint leaders and writers, including in general conference talks, reference Frankl's *Man's Search For Meaning* and, in particular, his assertion that "everything can be taken from a man but one thing: the last of human freedoms—to choose one's attitude in any given set of circumstances, to choose one's way."[46]

Frankl pioneered logotherapy in 1930, well before the Nazis imprisoned him (and his wife, parents, and siblings), and a good portion of logotherapy was based on attitudinal change. The term "attitude modification" was proposed in 1980 by Dr. Elisabeth Lukas, a student of Frankl's, as a way to contrast it with behavior modification that was becoming popular in American psychology in the 1970s.[47] The focus of the former was to emphasize that the first step toward behavioral change was to change a person's attitude. One of the four required classes to become a credentialed Diplomate Clinician in Logotherapy is titled "Attitudinal Change" and is focused on reframing thinking

---

46. For examples, see Wayne S. Peterson, "Our Actions Determine Our Character," *Ensign*, Nov. 2001, 83–84; James E. Faust, "Spiritual Healing," *Ensign*, May 1992, 6–8; and James E. Faust, "He Healeth the Broken in Heart," *Ensign*, July 2005, 2–7.

47. Elisabeth Lukas, "Modification of Attitudes," *International Forum for Logotherapy* 3 (1980): 25–35.

toward discovering meaning in life.[48] To underscore the power of attitudinal change, here is another quotation from Frankl of a reframed thought while behind the barbed wire fences of a Nazi concentration camp: "One evening, when we were already resting on the floor of our hut, dead tired, soup bowls in hand, a fellow prisoner rushed in and asked us to run out to the assembly ground and see the wonderful sunset. . . . After minutes of moving silence, one prisoner said to another, 'How beautiful the world could be!'"[49]

Frankl and his Jewish brothers focused their thoughts on the beautiful sunset even while starving to death in a prison. To repeat, "Everything can be taken from a man but one thing: the last of human freedoms—to choose one's attitude in any given set of circumstances, to choose one's own way."

Dr. Aaron Beck developed CBT in the early 1960s, and in 1994, he and his daughter, Dr. Judith Beck, founded the Beck Institute in Bala Cynwyd, Pennsylvania. While conducting experiments to validate the psychoanalytic concepts of depression (nexus of the pleasure principle and protest against society), Beck found no research support and instead proposed a new clinical approach to depression based on the concept of "automatic thoughts" about oneself, others, the world or society, and the future.[50] It is known as "cognitive behavior therapy" (CBT). In short, CBT maintains that a person's thoughts about situations (cognitions) largely determine their emotional and behav-

---

48. These four classes are explained at https://www.viktorfranklinstitute.org/educational-courses/.

49. Viktor Frankl, *Man's Search for Meaning* (Beacon Press, 2006), 59–60. Dr. Haddon Klingberg's authorized biography *When Life Calls Out to Us: The Love and Lifework of Viktor and Elly Frankl* (Image, 2002) is a book I highly recommend for anyone who wants tor learn more about Viktor Frankl's entire life.

50. For an excellent historical overview, see Aaron T. Beck, A. John Rush, Brian F. Shaw, and Gary Emery, *Cognitive Therapy of Depression* (The Guilford Press, 1987). To further understand CBT, I recommend Judith Beck, *Cognitive Behavior Therapy: Basics and Beyond*, 3rd ed. (The Guilford Press, 2020), or these two books by David Burns: *Feeling Great: The Revolutionary New Treatment for Depression and Anxiety* (PESI Publishing & Media, 2020) or *Feeling Good: The New Mood Therapy* (William Morrow Paperbacks, 1999). Burns was an early student of Aaron T. Beck.

ioral reactions. It is one of the most researched and evidenced-based practices used throughout mental health.

Today it is well known that certain types of mental disorders are rooted in very specific cognitive distortions. For example, people with anxiety will often have magnification and catastrophizing cognitive distortions in which they exaggerate the negativity of a situation (think of my past examples of when I have to call the plumber and automatically irrationally think of a considerable cost and then feel nervous). Perfectionists, who often struggle with anxiety and depression, will often have an all-or-nothing cognitive distortion, viewing themselves as "complete failures" because they received a 95 percent score on an exam in an undergraduate university class and will then ruminate on missing the 5 percent and begin to think they will have no future career and will embarrass their parents (combining all-or-nothing thinking with magnification and catastrophizing).

Prerequisites to CBT Reframing: Humility, Meekness, and Prayer

Lastly, before I explain the six common cognitive distortions in human thinking (linked to politics) and how to reframe such irrational thoughts, I'd like to share a little bit about the role of humility, meekness, and prayer in learning how to suspend and change our thoughts to listen to another person and understand them.

Reframing works well if it is based on humility, meekness, and prayer. Concerning the last concept, prayer, Alma 37:37 is deeply informative: "Counsel with the Lord in all thy doings, and he will direct thee for good." In chapters 3 Nephi 11–20, the power of prayer is taught and a total of eleven prayers are offered. And one of my favorite scriptures about prayer is Doctrine and Covenants 10:5: "Pray always, that you may come off conqueror; yea, that you may conquer Satan, and that you may escape the hands of the servants of Satan that do uphold his work."

I encourage you to use prayer as you try to reframe thoughts to understand those who think politically different than you and to reduce contention and conflict. Use prayer to help guide you toward identifying cognitive distortions and then reframing them. Prayer allows personal revelation on the topics discussed in the next section, such as how to use the double standard technique or what different political groups or people you want to contact to engage. Prayer can also help you gain personal revelation on how to respectfully ask someone about their political views that are different from yours, respectfully and honestly, to understand them through listening and building better relationships.

Regarding humility and meekness, the scriptures are the best teacher. Here are a few scriptures from the Bible and the Book of Mormon:

- Moses was very meek (see Numbers 12:3).
- The Lord dwells with those who are humble (see Isaiah 57:15).
- "He that shall humble himself shall be exalted" (Matthew 23:12).
- Jesus humbled Himself and became obedient unto death (see Luke 22:42; 23:46).
- "Humble yourselves in the sight of the Lord, and he shall lift you up" (James 4:10).
- "None is acceptable before God, save the meek and lowly in heart; and if a man be meek and lowly in heart, and confesses by the power of the Holy Ghost that Jesus is the Christ, he must needs have charity; for if he have not charity he is nothing; wherefore he must needs have charity" (Moroni 7:44).
- "And they were taught to walk humbly before the Lord; and they were also taught from on high" (Ether 6:17).
- "The meek shall inherit the earth" (Psalm 37:11; Matthew 5:5; 3 Nephi 12:5; Doctrine and Covenants 88:17).

A recent academic book written for the everyday person that was a *New York Times* bestseller is Dr. Adam Grant's *Think Again*, published in 2021. Dr. Grant posits that humility is a core feature of being a good thinker, including the "joy of being wrong."[51] He suggests that cognitive elasticity requires "extraordinary humility."[52]

---

51. Adam Grant, *Think Again: The Power of Knowing What You Don't Know* (Viking, 2021), 61
52. Adam Grant, *Think Again*, 52

Likewise, Elder Clark G. Gilbert stated:

> The most successful people are the humblest because they are confident enough to be corrected by and learn from anyone. Elder D. Todd Christofferson counseled us to "willingly [find ways] to accept and even seek correction." Even when things appear to be going well, we must seek out opportunities to improve through prayerful petition.[53]

Another gold nugget idea from Clayton M. Christensen is that "if you have a humble eagerness to learn something from everybody, your learning opportunities will be unlimited."[54] Humble eagerness is needed to locate and reframe cognitive distortions in yourself (again, not others).

Six Prevalent Cognitive Distortions in Political Thinking and How to Reframe Them

The number one role of our brain is to keep us alive. To do this, our brain is constantly looking for threats, and this role has been called the "threat response system" or "threat brain."[55] When humans lived in mud huts and wilderness settings, those threats were often poisonous snakes and bears, and those who lived longer constantly looked for such threats.

Today, in the United States, our threat brain is more focused on social media than poisonous snakes, or how a perceived political policy might affect us and the people we love. That is why the news and politicians constantly share negative events and stories; people

---

53. Clark G. Gilbert, "Becoming More in Christ: The Parable of the Slope," *Ensign* or *Liahona*, Nov. 2021. See also D. Todd Christofferson, "As Many as I Love, I Rebuke and Chasten," *Ensign* or *Liahona*, May 2011.

54. Clayton M. Christensen, "How Will You Measure Your Life?," Harvard Business Review, July–August 2010, https://hbr.org/2010/07/how-will-you-measure-your-life.

55. "How the brain gathers threat cues and turns them into fear," Salk Institute of Biological Studies, Aug. 16, 2022, https://www.salk.edu/news-release/how-the-brain-gathers-threat-cues-and-turns-them-into-fear/. See also Nelisha Wickremasinghe, "Is Your Threat Brain Always On? Why Our Survival Instinct Is Killing Us," *Psychology Today*, Nov. 30, 2020, https://www.psychologytoday.com/us/blog/spellbound/202011/is-your-threat-brain-always-on.

are more triggered by negative news than positive news because it can quickly turn on the brain threat. Sharing how the other political party or person will destroy a core value or tenet of a particular group (e.g., ethnicity, religion) if elected can fire up the base and activate people to head to the polls. But it also fires up fear and negativity via brain threat. Sadly, it can also create hatred for a particular cultural or political group.

Once a possible threat is perceived, the human brain provides an explanation—attributes of causation—to protect us. If we know the cause, we can then protect ourselves. Many times (but not always), our automatic fear and negative thoughts are not valid. But once there is a perceived threat—such as "if _____ is elected as president or governor, _____ [some horrible event] will happen"—we begin to see people who think differently as an enemy, sometimes even as an evil person, and our behaviors often move toward anger, resulting in yelling, threatening, and even fighting. Just like the magnification and catastrophizing cognitive distortions that enter my mind when I have a plumbing problem, magnification and catastrophizing begin (exaggerating the negativity) when we think _____ could be the next president, governor, senator, or mayor.

To help you capture the cognitive distortions within yourself, I ask you—my Latter-Day Saint brothers and sisters—to reflect on the many distortions that nonmembers have made about members of The Church of Jesus Christ of Latter-day Saints. Here are a few I have heard:

- Latter-day Saints do not believe in the Bible or Jesus Christ.
- Latter-day Saints worship Joseph Smith.
- Latter-day Saints are not Christians.

All are bugaboo or myths, and perhaps you are like me as I think, "How do people come to such faulty conclusions?" I also wish they would ask us what we believe. I suggest that most of us (but not all), as Latter-day Saints, do the same things when we engage in politics and dislike oppositional views—we believe myths and inaccurate views about other political parties and candidates. And it is not just us as Latter-day Saints that make such thinking errors; all cultural groups do this, including political affiliation groups (e.g., Republicans, Democrats, Libertarians, Green Party).

With this background, let's now turn to the six cognitive distortions linked specifically to political engagement. (Note that although they are explained as separate cognitive thinking errors, they often overlap.)[56]

COGNITIVE DISTORTION 1: ALL-OR-NOTHING THINKING

All-or-nothing thinking is a perception that is extremely black or white without seeing any shades of gray. It can be further delineated into positive all-or-nothing thinking and negative all-or-nothing thinking. In politics, this can occur when Democrats believe there are no excellent Republicans (and all Democrats are good) and Republicans think there are no good Democrats (and all Republicans are good). There are no shades of gray, such as there might be some fair-minded Republicans/Democrats.

All-or-nothing thinking is also closely coupled with the development of anxiety and anxiety disorders. This distorted thinking pattern propels individuals into a state of perpetual unease with related fear behaviors, such as avoiding people who think differently, experiencing anger, and then acting rude, discriminatorily, or violently toward others who think differently. A 2022 poll suggested that almost half of second-year college students reported that they would not choose to be roommates with someone who supported a different presidential candidate than they did in 2020. A majority reported they would not date someone who voted differently, and nearly two-thirds reported they could not view themselves marrying someone who backed a

---

56. Unless I reference otherwise, the six prevalent cognitive distortions and ways to reframe come from David Burn's 2020 book *Feeling Great: The Revolutionary New Treatment for Depression and Anxiety*, 209–302. Burns lists ten cognitive distortions and many more reframing techniques than I do in this book. However, his book is specifically focused on treatment for depression and anxiety, and I am using his cognitive distortion framework particularly in terms of political discourse. Scores of other books related to CBT list these same six cognitive distortions, such as *The Coddling of the American Mind* (2018) by Greg Lukianoff and Jonathan Haidt or *Cognitive Behavioral Therapy* (2021) by Judith Beck.

different presidential candidate two years prior. This is all-or-nothing tribalism, and it leads to conflict.

In my family, when the five of us (or six or seven, depending on who our sons are dating) sit around the dinner table on Sundays, we have incredibly different political views, and often we have rich discussions that have caused all of us to see the word differently and sometimes vote differently. My family is far from perfect, but we do this well, and I am deeply grateful for such conversations. To this end, friends often say, "I can't find a single thing that _____ [think of a past or current sitting American President, such as Donald Trump or Joe Biden] did that was good." To reframe, which means pausing between stimulus and response to reflect and evaluate automatic thoughts to learn if they might be irrational or in error, we need to challenge our thoughts directly.

"Should" and "must" statements make enormous demands (a hallmark feature of perfectionists), allow no shades of gray, are a form of all-or-nothing thinking,[57] and are also linked to people who struggle with depression and anxiety. In university life, this can occur when a student states or thinks, "I must get an A on the exam," and then feels intense disappointment in earning an A-, or when a student perseverates on missing one question when they correctly answered the other forty-nine questions.

Thirty-five years ago, when I first began to vote, I had this automatic thought that "I should follow the same voting patterns as my parents so they don't think I'm 'less than' and are disappointed in me." I had similar thoughts when thinking about my closest Christian friends. It caused intense emotional feelings when I began to explore different political parties and voted in a different way than my parents and many of my Church and Christian friends.[58]

---

57. In some CBT books, should-statements and all-or-nothing thinking are separate cognitive distortions, and in others other books they are joined.

58. To learn more of how I felt when I voted in a different way than my parents and many of my Church friends, see Rodney Dieser, "Perspective: Cognitive Rigidity Is Not an American Tradition Why Do We Act Like It Is?," *Deseret News*, Dec. 9, 2022, https://www.deseret.com/2022/12/9/23422660/cognitive-rigidity-partisanship-polarization-lincoln/.

The reframing technique used to change all-or-nothing thinking is called **thinking in shades of gray**. It's when you intentionally find some good things about the oppositional party and locate some of the not-so-good policies of the political party you align with. It takes humility and meekness to reframe well, which is why I find our family political conversations so meaningful. If you believe that Joe Biden or Donald Trump did nothing good when they were president, it means actively and honestly challenging this thought. I have lived in Iowa since 2001 and in Utah from 1991 to 1998. I have lived through the terms of many US presidents, and I can outline the strengths and weaknesses of each of them related to policies they moved forward.

Another way to reframe the thought "there is nothing good about the opposite party" (all-or-nothing thinking) is to respectfully **argue with yourself** by presenting accurate information on how an oppositional party is needed for a democracy to thrive.[59] Historian Annelien de Dijn's charting of democracy, beginning in some of the first democracies in ancient Greece, underscores the importance of oppositional parties (in robust governments including the United States of America) and how the elimination of the political opposition is what caused democracies to disappear. As one example, she showcases the rise and fall of ancient Rome's republican government (from 509 BCE to 27 BCE) and how liberty fell because of the killing off of people who served in opposition (e.g., Rome's seventh king, Lucius Tarquin).[60] On January 29, 2021, the *Deseret News* editorial board shared an opinion titled "What Happened to America's 'Loyal Opposition'?" with the

---

59. In the last chapter of this book, I will explain Dr. Richard Haass's ten habits of good citizens, which he calls the Bill of Obligations. Richard Haass is president of the nonpartisan Council on Foreign Relations. He has served as a diplomat and policymaker in the Pentagon, State Department, and White House under four presidents, both Democrat and Republican. His tenth habit of good citizens is "Put County First", and he outlines that democracy needs an opposition (and a free press) to keep the majority honest and create fertile ground for compromise.

60. Annelien de Dijn, *Freedom: An Unruly History* (Harvard University Press, 2020). To learn about the rise and fall of Roman liberty, see pages 69–125. To learn about Lucius Tarquin murdering his father-in-law, Servius Tullius, see pages 69–70 and 74.

subtitle "Our Extreme Partisanship Has Turned Fellow Americans into Enemies." The central message of this opinion piece is paramount: "When the loyal opposition dies . . . the soul of America dies with it."[61] The loyal opposition is legitimate, constructive, and responsible and is needed to hold the political party in power accountable. Democracy demands an oppositional party, and the hope is that it remains loyal to the nation's best interests. The oppositional party is not evil; it is foundational to democracy.

Another way to argue with yourself is to use **Socratic dialogue**, pioneered by Viktor Frankl and further developed by Arron Beck.[62] In this method of internal dialogue, you ask yourself a series of questions to help reevaluate or reframe a conclusion or construct new ideas. You can also ask yourself questions that show the irrationality and absurdity of what you are telling yourself. In its most dramatic form, you can pull out two (or more) chairs and sit in each chair to have a Socratic dialogue within yourself (in counseling, this is called the two-chair method, and each chair represents the competing view or value), but you can also have this internal discussion through worksheets, journaling, or reflection. Regarding my past irrational thought "I should follow the same voting patterns as my parents so they don't think I'm 'less than' and are disappointed in me," a counterargument (to oneself) could be "My parents also raised me to be an independent, self-reliant person, and part of independence is thinking differently than them. By disagreeing politically, I am making good on their value of wanting me to become an independent and self-reliant person. They may be upset if I told them I voted differently, but they will still love and accept me."

---

61. Deseret News Editorial Board, "What Happened to America's 'Loyal Opposition'? Our Extreme Partisanship Has Turned Fellow Americans Into Enemies," *Deseret News*, Jan. 29, 2021, https://www.deseret.com/opinion/2021/1/29/22249344/america-loyal-opposition-republicans-democrats-scott-rasmussen-division/.

62. Viktor Frankl, *Psychotherapy and Existentialism: Selected Papers on Logotherapy* (Simon & Schuster, 1967), 58; Burns, *Feeling Great*, 328–329; Beck, *Cognitive Behavior Therapy*, 10–11, 170–171. In contemporary logotherapy circles, Socratic dialogue is considered the "workhorse" of logotherapy, and in CBT circles it is viewed as the "cornerstone" of treatment.

Cognitive Distortion 2: Overgeneralization

Overgeneralization is when a person generalizes from a specific flaw, failure, or mistake to a broader entity (like a presidential candidate or a political party). In political events, you perceive a global pattern of negative based on a single event.

An overgeneralization is often detected when words like "always," "never", or "totally" are used. In political speak, it is a Republican who thinks that Democrats are "always" closed-minded and never open to hearing a Republican solution, or a Democratic who thinks the same thing about a Republican. A Pew Research study in 2019 clearly showed that most Republicans and Democrats think that the opposing party is more closed-minded than other Americans; 75 percent of Democrats thought that Republicans were closed-minded, and 64 percent of Republicans thought Democrats were closed-minded.[63] If a presidential candidate in one party makes an honest error—let's say they confuse dates or past events or get names confused about other leaders from different nations—it is stating something like "See, that person is totally incompetent," where a person generalizes from a specific mistake to making a judgment about their disposition or intelligence.

Another valuable reframing method for overgeneralization is the **double standard technique**, which means asking yourself if you would think the same way if your preferred candidate made the same mistake. For example, in the lead-up to the 2024 presidential election, both President Biden and former president Donald Trump mixed up the names of leaders of other nations. In a campaign speech in New Hampshire, Donald Trump confused the leaders of Turkey and Hungary, and during a press conference, President Biden confused the leaders of Mexico and Egypt. Republican media outlets mocked President Biden, and Democrat media outlets ridiculed Donald Trump. Neither media outlet mentioned much about their presidential hopeful making this same mistake.

---

63. "How Partisans View Each Other," Pew Research Center, Oct. 10, 2019, https://www.pewresearch.org/politics/2019/10/10/how-partisans-view-each-other/.

You can even extend the double standard technique by trying the **double standard technique with a self-disclosure** by asking yourself, "Have you ever confused the names of coworkers, relatives, or other people you know?" I can't speak about you, but I sometimes call my middle son (named Jonas) Zachary (the name of my youngest son). I have gotten names confused when talking about colleagues in other departments at the university campus where I have worked for twenty-three years.

Another reframing technique is the **semantic method**, which substitutes language (in your mind or when you communicate to others) that is less extreme. Instead of thinking "Republicans are totally violent gun lovers," a way to reframe would be to think "Republicans are strong advocates of second amendment rights." Instead of thinking "Democrats are environmental extremists," a way to reframe would be to think "Democrats are strong advocates of keeping God's creation beautiful." Reframing lowers negative emotions, increases prosocial behaviors (e.g., listening), and helps people see the positives in a political difference or debate.

Cognitive Distortion 3 and 4:
Mental Filter and Discounting the Positives

This cognitive distortion is when a person ignores the positives and focuses entirely on the negatives. In political events, this means focusing almost exclusively on the negatives of the opposing party or candidate and seldom noticing the positives. Although mental filters and discounting the positives are separate cognitive mistakes, they overlap tremendously.

One time, while driving from Cedar Falls to Cedar Rapids (both in Iowa), a one-hour drive, the person I was driving with, a devout Republican, stated this about President Obama: "He has been in power for six years. I can't find one thing that he has done well." Sadly, I can distinctly remember an ardent Democrat friend saying the same thing about George W. Bush. I am far from perfect, but I have never found a president (in the United States) or a prime minister (in Canada) to be that awful, and I can find good policy in parties that I have voted against.

Not only is discounting the positives simply inaccurate, but focusing on seeing the negative in another person (whether a close friend or the mayor of your city) will only cause negative energy and behaviors. Mental filtering and discounting the positives leads to confirmation bias,[64] which drives us to seek out information supporting our established position—finding story after story of the negative aspects of the person we do not want to be elected. We return, over and over, to the same websites, podcasts, and publications and to people who "speak our language," whether it's Rachel Maddow on MSNBC, Tucker Carlson on Fox News, or our friendship circles. The consequence is that politics becomes deeply tribal and conflict-driven.

The reframing technique that can help remedy this cognitive distortion is the **counting the positives** technique, where you intentionally find the positive actions or policies of the person or party that you do not want to win the election. To clients I see in counseling, I often call it "balancing the books," and I begin this counseling intervention by asking them if they know what accountants do. Usually, they look at me surprised, as this question seems to have come out of nowhere. But I explain that a good accountant balances the books and understands assets and liabilities. I tell them, "You need to fire the accountant in your mind who is only tracking the liabilities (of yourself or another person—in this context, someone running for political office you don't want to win) and replace them with an accountant who will pay attention to both the liabilities *and* the assets. You need to balance the books!

Likewise, many Americans in our hyperpartisan nation need to think like an accountant and keep track of the assets and liabilities of both political parties in a truly authentic and honest way. The gift of democracy demands this from us. As presidential historian Doris Kearns Goodwin underscored, the political genius of Abraham Lincoln was his ability to create the most unusual cabinet in history because he had the cognitive flexibility to consider cabinet members

---

64. Raymond Nickerson, "Confirmation Bias: A Ubiquitous Phenomenon in Many Guises," *Review of General Psychology* 2, no. 2 (1998): 175–220. Confirmation bias is the tendency of people to interpret, remember, and purposely seek out information that confirms their beliefs.

of different opinions and brought his disgruntled opponents and rivals together.[65] Constitutional historian Akhil Amar has noted that, like Lincoln, George Washington was renowned for his ability to listen to diverse thoughts and be willing to change his mind.[66] Lincoln and Washington were able to "balance the books" in their thinking.

Reframing and focusing on the positives was at the heart of President Lincoln's first inaugural address, "The Better Angels of Our Nature" (given March 4, 1861), in which he hoped that passion would give way to reason and that the Union would restore its luster in the eyes of a divided nation. Lincoln ended his address by saying, "We are not enemies but friends. We must not be enemies. Though passion may have strained us, it must not break our bonds of affection. The mystic chords of memory . . . will yet swell the chorus of the Union, when again touched, as surely, they will be, by the better angels of our nature."[67]

Cognitive Distortion 5: Jumping to Conclusions

The fifth distortion I'll discuss is when a person jumps to an upsetting conclusion that is not supported by facts.[68] In political events, it's when you assume you know what the political party or person you do not want to win is thinking (or their intentions) without having sufficient evidence.

There are two main types of conclusion-hopping that are not supported by facts. The first type is fortune telling, where a person makes a disturbing prediction about the future that is often negative and fear-based. Stated another way, a person will automatically believe

---

65. Doris Kearns Goodwin, *Team of Rivals: The Political Genius of Abraham Lincoln* (Simon & Schuster, 2006), xv–xix. Although this entire book needs to to read to understand Lincoln's cognitive flexibility to create the most unusual cabinet in history, the introduction of this book provides a good overview.

66. Akhil Reed Amar, *The Words That Made Us: America's Constitutional Conversations, 1760–1840* (Basic Books, 2021), 275–326.

67. You can read Lincoln's first inaugural address in the 2021 book *Abraham Lincoln: The Gettysburg Address and Other Works* (see pages 297–306).

68. A fact is information presented as having objective reality with trustworthy evidence. *Merriam-Webster.com Dictionary*, s.v. "fact," accessed Feb. 3, 2025, https://www.merriam-webster.com/dictionary/fact.

something not warranted by the facts and sometimes make up fabricated stories or data to support their fortune telling. Fortune telling is associated with a slippery slope argument (logic), in which an idea or course of action is predicted to lead to something unacceptable, wrong, or disastrous.

As it relates to mental health, fortune telling is the foundational cognitive distortion at the root of depression and anxiety. It might be a person with the automatic but chronic thought or prediction that "no one will ever love me or want to marry me" and then feels worthless. If someone asks them on a date, they might have the distorted predictive cognition, "I will make a complete fool of myself, and my date will know I'm nothing but a failure," which can cause them to feel anxiety just thinking about the upcoming date.

These same cognitive distortions—making a disturbing prediction about the future that is often negative and fear-based—are rampant during elections. I have heard, for thirty years, my Republican friends share that if Democrats get into office, something deeply, profoundly disastrous will occur. I have also listened to my Democrat friends jump to the same doomsday conclusions about Republican candidates and policies. Yet America keeps moving forward and none of these doomsday predictions have happened.

The second type of this jumping-to-conclusion cognitive error is mind reading, which occurs when a person believes they can somehow read the minds of others and know their intention and what they're thinking. An everyday example of mind reading is when a person is disappointed after giving a presentation to a group and has this automatic thought "Everyone thinks I am an idiot." Of course, we can't read the minds of others, so we really have no idea of what other people are thinking.

Regarding politics, one 2023 poll demonstrated how political mind reading works. While 91 percent of Republicans said they think it's very or extremely important that citizens should learn from the past to improve the country, only about a third of Democrats said they believed that to be true of GOP voters. These Democrat-minded people who were surveyed seemed to think they knew the minds and beliefs of Republicans yet were totally in error. Likewise, on the other side, while only 31 percent of Republicans say Democrats believe government accountability is very important or essential, 90 percent of Democrat respondents said they do believe in government accountability.[69]

The reframing technique that can help remedy mind reading is **inquiry**. This means asking people with whom you politically disagree, authentically and honestly, what they are thinking instead of jumping to conclusions (similar to what I shared earlier about wishing people would ask Latter-day Saints about their beliefs instead of assuming). Then, after you've asked them, listen—really, really listen. (Chapter 3 in this book will explain how to listen to someone to understand them.)

Take the policy of local school boards, for example. Instead of mind reading and believing that those who think teachers should be armed with guns in public schools are "wackos" secretly in cahoots with the National Rifle Association and like violence, that person may genuinely love children and legitimately believe this is a way to protect kids in schools. Likewise, in opposition, advocates who believe they can protect children in schools by arming teachers and training them to be accurate shooters can practice inquiry by asking teachers to share what they think about the subject. This can include asking the teachers in their communities and then truly listening, and it can also include reading research-based survey reports.

Inquiry can also include reading books written by political hopefuls, and doing so with an open mind to learn how they think (which may be difficult when you already dislike their policies and believe you can read their minds and already know how they think). Reading an entire book written by Joe Biden, Donald Trump, Hillary Clinton, Mitt Romney, Barack Obama, George W. Bush, or a presidential hopeful (e.g., Mike Pence, Elisabeth Warren)—or past governors, senators, or other government leaders (e.g., Senator Jeff Flank)—would

---

69. "The Left and Right Think They Live on Different Planets -- New Data Shows They're More Like Next-Door Neighbors," PR Newswire, June 14, 2023, https://www.prnewswire.com/news-releases/the-left-and-right-think-they-live-on-different-planets--new-data-shows-theyre-more-like-next-door-neighbors-301850742.html.

allow you to better understand how someone you may disagree with thinks politically.

Such reading is a democratic act in and of itself and underscores human dignity. (Abraham Lincoln was well known to have always been carrying a book and was seen reading whenever he had free time.)[70] Taking the time to read the ideas of someone you politically disagree with, and allow them to share their thoughts uninterrupted over hours (by you reading, say, hundreds of pages of their writing) is treating that person with high value and is an action of democracy.

Historically, think about the famous Lincoln–Douglas debates (August 21—October 15, 1858) where each of the seven debates lasted about three hours long![71] The structure of each debate had one candidate speaking for an hour, the other candidate speaking for an hour and a half, and the first candidate then rebutting for thirty minutes. People who attended often had to travel on horseback for hours. To understand the candidates (inquiry), much time was needed, and you had to hear the entirety of both candidates' opinions (not a one- or two-minute snippet summary on the news where the newscast-cherry picks the information they share). Inquiries might cause you to appreciate someone you don't like, or it might help you structure a counterargument that is civil and respectful rather than yelling and disrespectfully name-calling and ridiculing.

Examining the evidence is a reframing technique that can be used to prevent or remedy the cognitive distortion of fortune telling. In short, this strategy is locating case studies and research behind political claims you and others make in order to learn if such thoughts are accurate and trustworthy. Chapter 4 of this book will explain how to examine the evidence, such as finding case studies and research to evaluate competing claims. Has arming teachers prevented someone from entering a school with a gun or prevented them from killing kids and staff once they entered a school? Did such policies lead to unintended violence in schools?

---

70. Goodwin, *Team of Rivals*, 52.
71. Goodwin, *Team of Rivals*, 200–208.

Because fortune telling often leads to disastrous doomsday predictions (e.g., if this party wins the federal election, it will be suicidal for our nation), examining the evidence of how American democracy and governance works can also help reframe, calm people down, and create prosocial behavior. (Chapter 5 will suggest having schools teach more about American government and civics.) The US federal government has three branches: legislative, executive, and judicial. The legislative branch comprises the House and Senate, collectively called Congress, and the executive branch consists of the president, advisors, and various departments and agencies. Often, when a person believes that a certain president taking office will be disastrous, they don't understand that presidents rarely get to pass policies in the way they share them during the election campaign; instead, their ideas and policy initiatives usually become something different—something in the middle—due to the passing of laws and policies that have to go through both chambers of Congress. Then there is the judicial branch, which consists of the US Supreme Court, which influences laws. The American government system of checks and balances prevents disastrous one-sided or possible extreme positions, and a knowledge of this can put checks and balances on the cognitive distortion of fortune telling.

Creating a **cost-benefit analysis** is another reframing technique that explicitly targets fortune telling. It's when a person lists the advantages and disadvantages of voting one way versus another, such as whether schools should arm teachers or whether it's better to vote Republican or Democratic for the governor of your state. This is where a person, in an open-minded manner, hears both sides of an argument and makes a pros and cons list to try to make an educated decision.

I was naturalized as an American citizen in December 2022 and was excited to vote in my first federal election in November of 2024. However, I have voted in the federal Canadian election since I turned eighteen (through a special mail-in ballot for Canadian citizens living outside of Canada) and have always completed a cost-benefit analysis. (And I have voted for four different political parties in those elections.) The significance of knowing the various issues and policies of different political parties and then deciding on which are most important is captured well by President Oaks in his general conference talk titled "Defending Our Divinely Inspired Constitution":

> There are many political issues, and no party, platform, or individual candidate can satisfy all personal preferences. Each citizen must therefore decide which issues are most important to him or her at any particular time. Then members should seek inspiration on how to exercise their influence according to their individual priorities. This process will not be easy. It may require changing party support or candidate choices, even from election to election.
>
> Such independent actions will sometimes require voters to support candidates or political parties or platforms whose other positions they cannot approve. That is one reason we encourage our members to refrain from judging one another in political matters. We should never assert that a faithful Latter-day Saint cannot belong to a particular party or vote for a particular candidate. We teach correct principles and leave our members to choose how to prioritize and apply those principles on the issues presented from time to time. We also insist, and we ask our local leaders to insist, that political choices and affiliations not be the subject of teachings or advocacy in any of our Church meetings.[72]

Cognitive Distortion 6: Magnification and Minimization

Finally, there is the cognitive distortion of magnification and minimization. This refers to when a person exaggerates negativity and minimizes the positives. In political events, it's when you believe that what has happened or will happen (e.g., the opposing party's candidate wins the election) will be so awful that you (and possibly the entire nation) will not be able to stand it or survive it.

Magnification and minimization often overlap significantly with mental filters and discounting the positives. One time, when I was having relationship problems with a work colleague, I eventually realized that I magnified all his mistakes and minimized all the good things he was doing. My mind was good at pinpointing all of his errors, but it was not as sharp and precise in locating the good actions

---

72. Dallin H. Oaks, "Defending Our Divinely Inspired Constitution," *Ensign* or *Liahona*, May 2021, 108.

that he was taking at the university and with students in the classroom. When my colleague made a mistake, I blew things up and then tried to shrink and make invisible anything good that he did.

This same thing happens in political engagement. In real life, this plays out when a hardcore Republican will blow up the errors of Democrats but not those of their own political party and will minimize anything good that Democrats created or were involved in. And, of course, hardcore Democrats do the same with Republican leaders. Both can clearly see the hypocrisy in the *other* political party but not in their own.

Many of the reframing techniques already outlined—cost-benefit analysis, inquiry, counting the positive—can work to reframe magnification and minimization. However, two additional reframing techniques are **self-monitoring** and **exposure or contact**.

In the former, you keep track of your thoughts and look for patterns of magnification and minimization. Hopefully, you realize that part of your dislike of the other political party rests within your thinking errors. You may also recognize that you are still going to vote a certain way, but the other party is doing some good things.

The latter, exposure or contact, means hanging out with and engaging with the people you politically disagree with but in a genuinely open-minded manner. Some social and moral psychologists, such as Jonathan Haidt, posit that the best way to change our minds about politics is by interacting with other people (in good ways with no hostility) and by stepping out of our political tribal groups. Haidt states, "We are terrible at seeking evidence that challenges our own beliefs, but other people do us this favor, just as we are quite good at finding errors in other people's beliefs."[73] If you are a Democrat, this might mean attending political events of Republicans, not to debate and disrupt but to learn more about how they think, find more Republican-leaning friends in your community, and go and do fun things with them to develop healthy friendships so eventually you will be open to their ideas.

---

73. Jonathan Haidt, *The Righteous Mind: Why Good People Are Divided by Politics and Religion* (Vintage, 2012), 79.

Although ideologically different, it is well known that Justice Antonin Scalia and Justice Ruth Bader Ginsburg had mutual respect and a great friendship and bonded over a shared love of opera, food, and their childhoods in New York. Contact might mean seeing if there is a common ground or activity you can collaborate on—such as Republicans and Democrats working together to help a social cause. One historical example in the United States is the 1993 Religious Freedom Restoration Act signed into law by President Bill Clinton, something that came together through the combined efforts of Democrats and Republicans along with many religious groups and the ACLU.[74]

Conclusion

To listen to another person, especially a person who thinks politically different than you, the first step is to identify your automatic thoughts and reframe them so you can hear their voice and views and lower the stress you feel about it. The next chapter explains how to listen better, but again, you must first have the right mindset to listen.

Viktor Frankl developed the concept of reframing, but he viewed it as Socratic dialogue to change attitudes, with an axiom in which people can choose their attitude, even in the most desperate and dire circumstances. Aaron Beck pioneered CBT, which maintains that a person's thoughts about situations (cognitions) largely determine their emotional and behavioral reactions. CBT is one of the most researched and evidenced-based practices used throughout the world of mental health. Reframing is the ability to pause between stimulus and response to identify automatic thoughts and then evaluate them to see if they are irrational. As a review, the twelve reframing techniques explained in this chapter are as follows:

1. Thinking in shades of gray—Intentionally find some good things about the oppositional party and locate some of the not-so-good policies of the political party you align with.

---

74. To learn more about the passage of this bill, see Religious Freedom Restoration Act of 1993 at Congress.gov: https://www.congress.gov/bill/103rd-congress/house-bill/1308.

2. Arguing with yourself—Present accurate information on how an oppositional party is needed for a democracy to thrive and see its role as keeping the party in power accountable.
3. Socratic dialogue—Through internal dialogue, ask yourself a series of questions to help reevaluate or reframe a conclusion or construct new ideas. You can also ask yourself questions that show the irrationality and absurdity of what you're telling yourself.
4. Double standard technique—Ask yourself if you would think the same way if your preferred candidate made the same mistake as the candidate you oppose and have criticized.
5. Double standard technique with a self-disclosure—Ask yourself if you would think the same way if you made the same mistake as the candidate you oppose and have criticized.
6. Semantic method—Substitute less extreme language (in your mind or when communicating with others).
7. Counting the positives—Intentionally find the positive actions or policies of the person or party that you do not want to win the election.
8. Inquiry—Ask people you politically disagree with, genuinely and honestly, what they are thinking and then listen to their views with an open mind.
9. Examining the evidence—Locate case studies and research behind political claims you and others make to learn if such thoughts are accurate and trustworthy. This can also include obtaining an accurate understanding of how the American government is structured and how it functions.
10. Cost-benefit analysis—List the advantages and disadvantages of voting one way versus another.
11. Self-monitoring—Track your thoughts, look for patterns of cognitive distortions (e.g., magnification and minimization), and hopefully realize that part of the reason you dislike the other political party rests within your own thinking errors.
12. Exposure or contact—Hang out with and engage with people you politically disagree with, but do so in a truly open-minded manner. In addition, read their publications and watch their newscasts and social media platforms. Contact might mean

seeing if there is a common ground or activity that you can team up together on, such as Republicans and Democrats working together to help a social cause.

3
Listening to Understand Instead of Listening to Argue

I AM SURE YOU HAVE FELT GOOD KNOWING SOMEONE HAS TRULY heard you. I know I have. One time, when I was in high school, I made a reasonably large mistake, and when I went to one of my teachers to offer an authentic apology and share why I did what I did, he took the time to truly hear my voice. It was a genuine experience, and a bond was built between us. It was an experience that transformed me.

The title of this chapter is the thesis; the goal is to have you, the reader, learn how to listen to hear another person and understand them, not to listen to another person to argue with them. Listening to understand starts with a mindset, and the previous chapter explained how to create such a mindset. Being curious about another person's thoughts and believing you can learn and grow from them is a good mindset for political dialogue. To draw from Braver Angels, a nonprofit dedicated to decreasing political depolarization, listening to people we politically disagree with should be anchored to honesty, dignity, and respect.[75]

Listening to understand is based on "strong-sense critical/reflective thinking" and not what is known as "weak-sense critical/reflective thinking."[76] Weak-sense critical/reflective thinking entails using curiosity, listening, and thinking skills to confirm a bias or serve an often hidden and confrontational agenda, such as to win a debate or argument or to shame and humiliate the other person. Another agenda that's often linked to weak-sense critical/reflective thinking might be to hide the hypocrisy of oneself or one's political party. Strong-sense critical/reflective, on the other hand, uses curiosity, listening, and thinking skills to learn and understand other viewpoints and to have insights into our own (not others') cognitive and affective processes.

Having taught reflective thinking skills (including how to listen) for over twenty years at the university level, I have witnessed too many students who learn higher-order thinking and listening skills, only to then use them against others and for the sake of winning arguments rather than on themselves and for the sake of learning and growing. I have also witnessed this in marriage and couples therapy. Often, when a couple embarks on relationship therapy, they are keenly aware of their partner's weaknesses and struggles. However, they rarely use this same critical or reflective eye on their own behaviors or cognitive distortions. They can quickly note how their spouse is not listening to them and can be quick to critique them, but they have a hard time seeing this in themselves. Occasionally, I will engage with a couple who can critique themselves and are aware that their relationship can improve by focusing on changing their own behaviors and attitudes, often acknowledging that they need to listen better to their spouse. When the latter happens, marriages and relationships become better.

Before I explain listening actions or skills you can develop, I want to share ten wonderful quotations I've heard about listening, and then

---

75. See https://braverangels.org/our-mission/.
76. I draw from M. Neil Browne and Stuart M. Keeley's book *Asking the Right Questions: A Guide to Critical Thinking* (the 12th edition from 2017), 1–10.

I'll share one of the best general conference talks I have heard about listening.

1. "The word 'listen' contains the same letters as the word 'silent.'" (Alfred Brendel)[77]
2. "We have two ears and one mouth, so we should listen more than we say." (Zeno of Citium)[78]
3. "This is the problem with dealing with someone who is actually a good listener. They don't jump in on your sentences, saving you from actually finishing them, or talk over you, allowing what you do manage to get out to be lost or altered in transit. Instead, they wait, so you have to keep going." (Sarah Dessen)[79]
4. "Listen with curiosity. Speak with honesty. Act with integrity. The greatest problem with communication is we don't listen to understand. We listen to reply. When we listen with curiosity, we don't listen with the intent to reply. We listen for what's behind the words. . . . Sometimes all a person wants is an empathetic ear; all he or she needs is to talk it out. Just offering a listening ear and an understanding heart for his or her suffering can be a big comfort." (Roy T. Bennett)[80]
5. "To say that a person feels listened to means a lot more than just their ideas get heard. It's a sign of respect. It makes people feel valued." (Deborah Tannen) [81]
6. "Too often we underestimate the power of a touch, a smile, a kind word, a listening ear, an honest compliment, or the

---

77. Alfred Brendel is a Czech-born Austrian classical pianist, poet, author, composer, and lecturer.
78. Zeno of Citium was a Hellenistic philosopher from Citium, Cyprus. He was the founder of the Stoic school of philosophy, which he taught in Athens beginning approximately in 300 BC.
79. Sarah Dessen is an American novelist.
80. Roy T. Bennett was an American attorney, CPA, and political executive who was the chairman of the Ohio Republican Party from 1988 to 2009 and again in 2012 and 2013.
81. Deborah Frances Tannen is a Georgetown University American author and linguistics professor.

smallest act of caring, all of which have the potential to turn a life around." (Leo Buscaglia)[82]
7. "If we can share our story with someone who responds with empathy and understanding, shame can't survive." (Brené Brown)[83]
8. "There's a lot of difference between listening and hearing." (G. K. Chesterton)[84]
9. "When you talk, you are only repeating what you already know. But if you listen, you may learn something new." (Dalai Lama)[85]
10. The most basic of all human needs is the need to understand and be understood. The best way to understand people is to listen to them." (Ralph G. Nichols)[86]

When the federal political election season kicks off in the United States, you rarely see anyone listening to someone who has different political views. Rather, you tend to see actions that are more like a ten-year-old having a temper tantrum, lots of pointing fingers at others, and aggressive name-calling. Extremely sad and harmful is the fact that even listening has been viewed as displaying weakness. As I shared in the previous chapter, 59 percent of Americans find political conversations with those they disagree with as "stressful and frustrating," up 9 percent since 2019.[87]

---

82. Felice Leonardo Buscaglia was an American author, motivational speaker, and professor at the University of Southern California.
83. Brené Brown is an American professor, social worker, author, and podcast host.
84. Gilbert Keith Chesterton was an English author, philosopher, Christian apologist, and literary and art critic.
85. The incumbent Dalai Lama is the highest spiritual leader and head of Tibetan Buddhism.
86. Ralph G. Nichols was the founder and first president of the International Communication Association and a professor at the University of Minnesota.
87. Ted Van Green, "Republicans and Democrats Alike Say It's Stressful to Talk Politics with People Who Disagree," Pew Research Center, Nov. 23, 2021, https://www.pewresearch.org/short-reads/2021/11/23/republicans-and-democrats-alike-say-its-stressful-to-talk-politics-with-people-who-disagree/.

Counsel from Latter-day Saint Leaders and Sources on Listening

Today, President Russell M. Nelson serves as the prophet of The Church of Jesus Christ of Latter-day Saints. Years earlier, while serving as an Apostle, he gave a general conference address on listening that is as applicable today as it was back in 1991.

He begins his talk by referencing the invocation for the Saturday afternoon conference session, given by Elder Hugh W. Pinnock who prayed that "we might listen carefully." President Nelson then outlines many articles in Church literature written on the "important art of listening" and cites Proverbs 19:20: "Hear counsel, and receive instruction, that thou mayest be wise." His talk is broken into how to listen from six different perspectives—children, parents, partners, neighbors, Church leaders, and the Lord—but there's a phrase that's repeated over and over under these six perspectives: "Learn to listen, then listen to learn from ____" (children, parents, partners, neighbors, Church leaders, and the Lord).

When it comes to listening to children, he shares the following:

A wise father once said, "I do a greater amount of good when I listen to my children than when I talk to them."

When our youngest daughter was about four years of age, I came home from hospital duties quite late one evening. I found my dear wife to be very weary. I don't know why. She only had nine children underfoot all day. So I offered to get our four-year-old ready for bed. I began to give the orders: "Take off your clothes; hang them up; put on your pajamas; brush your teeth; say your prayers" and so on, commanding in a manner befitting a tough sergeant in the army. Suddenly she cocked her head to one side, looked at me with a wistful eye, and said, "Daddy, do you own me?"

She taught me an important lesson. I was using coercive methods on this sweet soul. To rule children by force is the technique of Satan, not of the Savior. No, we don't own our children. Our parental privilege is to love them, to lead them, and to let them go.

The time to listen is when someone needs to be heard. Children are naturally eager to share their experiences, which range from triumphs of delight to trials of distress. Are we as eager to listen?

If they try to express their anguish, is it possible for us to listen openly to a shocking experience without going into a state of shock ourselves? Can we listen without interrupting and without making snap judgments that slam shut the door of dialogue? It can remain open with the soothing reassurance that we believe in them and understand their feelings. Adults should not pretend an experience did not happen just because they might wish otherwise.[88]

When it comes to listening to spouses—what President Nelson called "partners"—he tells this humorous story that has a significant lesson on listening:

> Husbands and wives, learn to listen, and listen to learn from one another. I was amused to read of an experience recorded by Elder F. Burton Howard in his biography of President Marion G. Romney: "His good-humored love for Ida was manifested in many ways. He delighted in telling of her hearing loss. 'I once went to see a doctor about her hearing,' he would say. 'He asked me how bad it was, and I said I didn't know. He told me to go home and find out. The doctor instructed me to go into a far room and speak to her. Then I should move nearer and nearer until she does hear. Following the doctor's instructions, I spoke to her from the bedroom while she was in the kitchen—no answer. I moved nearer and spoke again—no answer. So I went right up to the door of the kitchen and said, "Ida, can you hear me?" She responded, "What is it, Marion—I've answered you three times."'"[89]

He also addresses listening to our neighbors when there are political and religious differences. He starts this section of his talk by referencing Leviticus 19:18 and Matthew 19:19 when the Lord said, "Thou shalt love thy neighbor." He then states:

> Opportunities to listen to those of diverse religious or political persuasion can promote tolerance and learning. And a good listener will listen to a person's sentiments as well. I learned much from Brother David M. Kennedy as we met with many dignitaries in nations abroad. When one of them spoke, Brother Kennedy not only looked eye to eye and listened with real intent, but he even

---

88. Russell M. Nelson, "Listen to Learn," *Ensign*, May 1991, 22.
89. Russell M. Nelson, "Listen to Learn," 23.

removed his reading glasses, as if to show that he wanted nothing in the way of his total concentration. The wise listen to learn from neighbors.

President Nelson ends his talk by positing, "Above all, God's children should learn to listen, then listen to learn from the Lord." During the Church's special birthday broadcast to honor President Nelson's 100th birthday (broadcasted on September 9, 2024), Elder Oaks disclosed how he admires how Present Nelson engages with councils and committees by first asking others to respond before making decisions.[90] That is, he listens first!

There are many good Latter-day Saint talks on listening. Still, one of my personal favorites is Elder Holland's October 2016 conference talk titled "Emissaries to the Church," in which he tells the heart-wrenching story of how his friend, Troy Russell, pulled his pickup truck slowly out of his garage on his way to donate goods to the local Deseret Industries and accidentally drove over, and killed, his precious nine-year-old son, Austen. Elder Holland shares the emotional pain of Troy Russell—a pain I cannot fathom. He also shares how John Manning, "home teacher extraordinaire," spent time ministering to Troy Russell by taking him each morning to play basketball at the local church. However, the basketball was not what was important; it was what John Manning did driving to the church and back, and often sitting in their vehicle for hours in the parking lot: "From that first day back, we talked—or rather I talked, *and John listened.*"[91]

Here is another wonderful talk on listening that I find profoundly moving: "Taking Time to Talk and Listen" by President Rosemary M. Wixom. Here is one gold nugget of truth and wisdom she shared:

> When we listen, we see into the hearts of those around us. Heavenly Father has a plan for each of His children. Imagine if we could get a glimpse of the individual plan for each of our children. What if we could know how to enhance their spiritual gifts? What if we could know how to motivate a child to reach his or her potential? What

---

90. "President Nelson's 100th Birthday Celebration" (video), Gospel Library.
91. Jeffrey R. Holland, "Emissaries to the Church," *Ensign* or *Liahona*, Nov. 2016, 67; emphasis added.

if we could know how to help each child transition from childlike faith to testimony?

How can we know?

We can begin to know by listening.[92]

Two scriptures that underscore the importance of listening are James 1:19—"Wherefore, my beloved brethren, let every man be swift to hear, slow to speak, slow to wrath"—and Proverbs 18:13—"He that answereth a matter before he heareth it, it is folly and shame unto him."

George Washington as the Listener in Chief

George Washington and Abraham Lincoln are the two greatest presidents in American history. Whether conducted by political scientists, historians, or the general population, George Washington is often ranked as America's greatest president, followed by Abraham Lincoln. As I have studied these two men, and read many books about them from noted and distinguished historians and constitutional scholars, it is clear that both leaders had cognitive elasticity—which means they were open-minded and had the ability to consider different perspectives and opinions—and because of this, they became brilliant in making very tough and consequential decisions (like what President Oaks shared about President Nelson's ability to listen to the views of others when working with councils and committees). As I studied George Washington and Abraham Lincoln, I realized that their cognitive agility was linked to their ability to listen, and modern-day research underscores that listening and being open-minded are interrelated and contribute to good decision-making. Dr. Amar's extensive research tells us that during America's constitutional conversation, Washington was "an outstanding listener. He absorbed information well. . . . Adams loved to talk, but often failed to listen. Jefferson wore ideological blinders, and routinely took in only what he wanted to take in. Washington excelled at soliciting and processing advice

---

92. Rosemary M. Wixom, "Our Homes, Our Families: Taking Time to Talk and Listen," *Ensign*, Apr. 2012, 36.

and information from a broad range of sources. At the Philadelphia Convention, he was indeed *the listener in chief*."[93]

Washington demonstrated military competence and valor, but what is often overlooked is that he also had auditory proficiency and an open mind. In the superb 2010 Pulitzer Prize winner *Washington: A Life*, when it came to interactions with revolutionary war generals and war councils, Chernow calls Washington a "peerless listener," a war commander who never made lightning-fast decisions and "made excellent use of war councils to weigh all sides of an issue, . . . usually groped his way to firm and accurate conclusions, . . . [and] was at his best when reacting to options presented by others."[94] As Dr. Amar adds, Washington was a voracious reader, "scourging every piece of printed information he could find" and "pondering speeches and writing on both sides of the [ratification] question. Washington himself had been emphatically on one side—the yes side—but he understood there was another side, and further understood that there were many honorable people and many honorable arguments on that side."[95]

Dr. Edward Larson's book, *The Return of George Washington*—which tells the story of Washington from his resignation as commander in chief through his inauguration as president—provides many examples of how Washington read and listened to others[96] ("reading" is a form of listening that will be explained in greater depth in the last chapter of this book).

Larson outlined that Washington was constantly seeking out the advice of peers through letters, such as when he reached out to David

---

93. Akhil Reed Amar, *The Words That Made Us: America's Constitutional Conversations, 1760–1840* (Basic Books, 2021), 303; emphasis added.
94. Ron Chernow, *Washington: A Life* (Penguin Books, 2011), 272, 292.
95. Amar, *The Words That Made Us*, 307.
96. Edward J. Larson is a professor of history and holds the distinguished Hugh & Hazel Darling Chair in Law at Pepperdine University (and is a winner of the Pulitzer Prize for his past academic labor in history).

Humphreys[97] and Henry Knox[98] regarding whether he should attend the Constitutional Convention in Philadelphia and then endorsed the government reform proposals both men made via correspondence related to the creation of the Constitution. Washington then called on James Madison[99] for additional advice and listened acutely. As soon as Washington arrived in Philadelphia, he called on Benjamin Franklin,[100] and these two men spent much time in face-to-face conversation. (Despite their reciprocal admiration because Franklin spent most of the war in France and Washington was in the military field, the two men barely knew each other except by reputation.) Larson notes that during the Constitutional Convention in Philadelphia, Washington listened to and relied heavily on the scholarly and legal thinking of James Madison, Gouverneur Morris,[101] and James Wilson,[102] and he listened to Knox and Madison about John Adams serving as the first vice president. Washington listened profoundly to David Humphreys when drafting his inaugural address. Of course,

---

97. David Humphreys was an American Revolutionary War colonel, aide de camp to George Washington, and secretary and intelligence agent for Benjamin Franklin in Paris.

98. Henry Knox is a Founding Father of the United States. He was a Boston bookseller who became a senior general of the Continental Army during the Revolutionary War and served as chief of artillery in most of Washington's campaigns.

99. James Madison was an American statesman, diplomat, and Founding Father who served as the fourth president of the United States from 1809 to 1817.

100. Benjamin Franklin is one of the foremost Founding Fathers, as he was the only man to sign the three critical documents at the birth of the United States: the Declaration of Independence, the Treaty of Paris, and the Constitution. He was also known as a political philosopher, author, inventor, scientist, and diplomat. As part of the subject of listening, Franklin formed a biweekly discussion group on the topic of republican government before the Constitutional Convention.

101. Gouverneur Morris was a Founding Father of the United States and a signatory to the Articles of Confederation and the United States Constitution. He wrote the preamble to the United States Constitution and is often called the "Penman of the Constitution."

102. James Wilson was a Founding Father, legal scholar, jurist, and statesman who served as an associate justice of the United States Supreme Court from 1789 to 1798.

President Washington listened to Alexander Hamilton,[103] and it is well known that Washington received and read newspapers from around the country daily and then commented and asked for comments in his massive private correspondence. (It is also well known that Abraham Lincoln did the same.) Washington was constantly listening, which is why one of the most significant Constitutional scholars of our time—Dr. Akhil Reed Amar—called him "the listener in chief."

Active Listening and the Skill Sets of Listening

I want to share a story of an argument my good wife and I had many years ago when I was a doctoral student at the University of Alberta in Canada. Ricki was to pick me up at the east door of the institute building on the University of Alberta campus in the late afternoon. That is what I thought, but Ricki remembered me asking her to pick me up at the west door. This was in the late 1990s with no cell phones. We both waited almost an hour on the other side of the building. What is now so humorous (though it wasn't at the time) is that this is not a big building! But we both waited and waited. We both thought we may have misunderstood, and we both walked around the building looking for the other. We realized later, when we spoke about this event, that we actually walked around the building at the exact same time!

When we finally found each other, we were both upset and believed the other had misunderstood. I kept saying, "Ricki, I said the east door, not the west door." Ricki responded, "No, Rod, you have it backward; you said the west door, not the east door." Just missing a few words can cause much misunderstanding and confusion, and modern-day research suggests that when people speak, they may only understand about 20 percent accurately. If we want to develop positive relationships with people who politically think differently than we do, it takes a tremendous amount of energy and internal strength to listen to understand, as even a few misunderstood words can lead to a state of confusion.

---

103. Alexander Hamilton was an American military officer, statesman, and Founding Father who served as the first US treasury secretary from 1789 to 1795 during George Washington's presidency.

Listening is a skill set that can be learned, similar to a skill set that must be mastered before playing a sport. For example, to play basketball, a person would need to learn these skills: dribbling, shooting, passing, rebounding, jumping, footwork, and defense. Likewise, to listen, a person needs to learn these action skills: paraphrasing, clarifying, reflecting, summarizing, probing, information-giving, interpretation, and confrontation. At its most basic level, listening involves understanding the message conveyed to you through sound waves and then responding to it. At a more advanced level, it consists of understanding the emotional aspects linked to the message conveyed to you through sound waves and then responding to it.

The word *active* means engagement or pursuing an activity, and active listening means pursuing activities to help you understand what another person has communicated to you. To listen well, a person needs to focus 100 percent of their attention on the other person and not become distracted by internal thoughts, such as wondering about a work task, being distracted by a thought like "He has no idea what he's talking about," or thinking about what you'd like to eat later in the day. Listening well also means not being distracted by external stimuli, such as pinging notifications from a smartphone or children running around in the background. A good mindset when entering into a conversation with someone, whether political or not, is to say to yourself, "I want to repeat back to the person what they said and hope they say, 'You got it!'" Often, when I work with people in couples and marriage therapy, I ask them how they listen at work, and most people respond by saying they repeat back what was said to them. I then ask if they can use this skill set in their marriage as well.

Although there are some paramount cross-cultural differences, listening well requires looking at another person without doing anything else and letting them share their views.

Active listening means asking questions to understand better, not questions to cast doubt or to critique. Paramount is "questioning with curiosity," as it shows authentic and genuine interest and fosters deeper conversation and understanding for both parties. It often creates positive relationship bonds since being heard by another person is a rewarding and positive experience; we all feel good when we know someone has genuinely heard us. Questioning with curiosity helps uncover the meaning behind what is being shared and can lead to emotional understanding, such as realizing that this person believes so strongly in teachers having guns in schools (or schools becoming places that are gun-free) because they love their children deeply and want to protect them. As a general rule, interrupting during conversations often suggests underdeveloped listening skills. Listening also connotes "holding space" for the other person to talk without having your own internal agenda, and extremely good listeners hear other people's emotions too, such as sadness, fear, hope, anger, or passion.

Every mental health counseling graduate training program has a class dedicated to helping counselors in training learn how to listen to understand. Often the class is called "Counseling Skills" and teaches the micro-skills or fundamental skills of listening. It is usually taught in the very first semester when new graduate students begin working on their master's degree. I remember vividly taking such a class at the University of Utah when I first embarked on a professional counseling career, and we spent the entire class learning the action skills of listening presented below. These foundational listening skills are the bedrock of further courses and are foundational throughout a counselor's career. Below, I explain the eight fundamental skills of listening (also known as actions of listening) and provide a political issue-based example for each.

Paraphrasing: Repeating back the content of the speaker's message in your own words to better understand the content. Often, this begins with "If I'm hearing you right, you're saying that . . ." or "Let me make sure I understand by repeating back. You're saying that . . ."

An example could be "If I'm hearing you right, you're saying that you believe that the Religious Freedom Restoration Act is an important law because it strengthens religious rights in our state. Do I have this correct?" A policy inverse example would be "If I'm hearing you right, you're saying that the Religious Freedom Restoration Act should be halted because it will allow prejudice to go unchecked and could be dangerous for certain communities that have majority religions that won't allow minority religions to be heard. Do I have this correct?"

Clarification: Encouraging the speaker to elaborate or checking the accuracy of what you think the speaker said. Often this begins with "Do you mean that . . ." or "Are you saying that . . ." followed by a rephrasing of the other person's message.

An example is "Are you saying that you don't believe in student loan forgiveness plans because you believe it's not fair for people who didn't go on to university to pay for other people to go on to university and gain a degree? Can you tell me more?" If the speaker believed in a student loan forgiveness plan, an example of clarification could be "Are you saying that you believe in a student loan forgiveness plan because you think such a policy helps people who are poorer (who have higher student debt) pay off their loans so that then they can spend more money on home ownership and, in turn, help the economy grow? Can you tell me more?"

Reflection: Rephrasing the affective (emotional) part of the client's message to understand emotions better. In many ways, reflection is similar to paraphrasing but is very different because you want to focus on understanding their feelings, not the content.

An example could be "What I'm gathering is that your fear goes down knowing that there are teachers in your school who are trained in using guns to stop an intruder that might enter the school to kill children. Do I have this right?" Or "What I'm gathering is that your fear goes down knowing that schools are gun-free zones because this can prevent guns from falling into the wrong hands and prevent more gun violence in schools. Do I have this right?"

Summarization: Condensing the person's message, into two or more sentences, to synthesize common themes. It often involves combining reflection and paraphrasing to understand complex content connected to emotions.

Here's an example: "If I'm hearing you right, it sounds like you're voting for the Democratic candidate for many reasons, including their stance on government involvement. You see government involvement as a way to increase liberty and freedom among poorer people, and you feel hopeful and happy knowing that America is still a place where a person can go from rags to riches and live the American dream. The government helps in this. Am I capturing this right?" And here's an example with the opposite political ideology: "If I'm hearing you right, it sounds like you're voting for the Republican candidate for many reasons, including their stance on less government involvement. You see government involvement as a way that decreases liberty and handcuffs hardworking Americans in many ways, such as in higher taxes. You feel hopeful and happy knowing that America is still a place where a person can go from rags to riches and live the American dream. The government gets in the way of this. Am I capturing this right?"

Probing: Encouraging elaboration with simple, open-ended questions. It often begins with "Tell me more about . . ."

Using the situation above, here are two examples: "Can you tell me more about how you see government involvement supporting the American dream among the poor?" Or "Can you tell me more about how you see government involvement interfering in the pursuit of the American dream?"

Information-giving (listening through open-minded questioning): Asking the speaker to provide more information on the topics at hand, such as requesting to see links or research evidence for their position. The key to information giving is to ask questions in an authentic and genuine manner. Counterfeit questions are disguised attempts to send a counter message (listening to win an argument rather than listening to understand).

Here's an example of asking a question for additional information: "As you know, I'm pro-life and am against most types of abortion, with the exception of rape and when a mother's life is in danger. I've heard you say that abortions decrease and adoptions increase when women have the right to choose. I have to say that I've never heard of this before and am suspicious about it. Would you send me some links that provide statistical evidence of this? I want to look at this with an open mind."

Interpretation: Sharing a possible explanation of the speaker's message. The key is to offer an interpretation tentatively rather than as absolute fact.

Here's an example: "I think what's bothering you is how [political candidate] treats veterans, in both words and policy. What do you think?"

Confrontation (or challenge): Describe a discrepancy or mixed messages in the speaker. Of all the listening responses, this is the one that, if done incorrectly, can harm or undercut any positive relationship, as the speaker may believe you're betraying them. (Because of this, I hesitated even including this listening response in this book.) It should only be used when you have a very good and long relationship with someone who has a different political view than you. It has to be delivered humbly, with genuineness.

Here's an example: "Bill, I'm genuinely not understanding, and it may be that I didn't hear you right, but I'm tripped up on what could be a mixed message. On the one hand, I hear you say that you're against the war in Ukraine and that the United States needs to stop supplying weapons of war to Ukraine. Yet on the other hand, I'm hearing you say that President Putin in Russia is an evil dictator who is antidemocratic. How do you put these two together? Help me understand."

A Hypothetical Example of Using Listening Skills in a Political Conversation

Below is an example of a political conversation between two fictional characters, Bill and Ron, that demonstrates the listening skills we just covered. The conversation is about government-based national health care (a single-payer system) in the United States.

Bill: I have to tell you, Ron, that I disagree with you about national health care. I'm in favor of it, but I know that you're not. If I promise to listen and not get into an argument, would you mind telling me some of the reasons you oppose national health care?

Ron: Sure, Bill. Much of it rests with what our Founding Fathers believed—that America is best when there's less government. It's not the government's role to make sure everyone who wants health insurance can get it, and I see this as a huge step toward socialism.

Bill: I want to make sure I understand. At your core, you believe America is best when there's less government. And the reason you oppose national health care rests with your view of free enterprise as a core American value. *(Paraphrase)*

Ron: Yes, you got it! Europeans believe in socialism. And we're Americans! I realize there's a big difference between democratic socialism—like what they have in Sweden, where the people want and vote for big government—and communism, as you see in China. However, our Founding Fathers wanted America to be different from Europe, and they believed in free markets because free markets allow us to have greater freedom—freedom of choice and not having the government dictate what health care covers and does not.

Bill: [Bill wants to disagree with Ron because he views George Washington and Alexander Hamilton as advocates of an important federal and central government. But he promised to listen to Ron, so he bites my tongue.] Can you tell me more about how you see private enterprises creating greater health care choices? In countries like Canada, I believe they have as much choice as we have. I want to understand your thinking better. *(Clarification)*

Ron: I'm not sure Canada has as many choices as we do. Each of Canada's provinces has one government plan. I want a choice between different health care plans that we can opt into so I can find one that works for me and my family. In addition, taxation is so high in Canada because they pay a substantial amount of money for health care through taxes, which then takes away our choices when we have more discretionary funds. Also, there's so much waste since once people are given free health care, they'll abuse it by going to doctors for every little thing. In America, we learn self-reliance and how to be responsible for our own health.

Bill: So there are many reasons you prefer privatization of health care in America. First, it fits the value ethos of the Founding Fathers. Second, you feel that you and other Americans have more choice and freedom in finding health care insurance tailored to you, whereas a one-size-fits-all wouldn't be tailored to your specific needs. Third, you see waste as a consequence, and that waste of seeing doctors when you don't need to contributes to high taxes and wasteful government spending. Do I have this right? *(Summarization)*

Bill: You got it! And two more things: Look at the government-run Department of Veterans Affairs. It's an example of a totally failed system. Compare that to the Mayo Clinic, the best in the world. I also like how nonprofits, like the Mayo Clinic, are nongovernment health care organizations, but as nonprofits, they reinvest all earnings into giving patients high-quality care. And second, linked to that, competition is how to keep costs down, and you can have nonprofits, like the Mayo Clinic, compete with for-profit health care. This is a case where a nonprofit wins out and has the best care in the world. I love the idea of nonprofit-driven health care—it's way better than for-profit health care and still allows competition in the markets!

Bill: I just wanted to better understand the first part of what you said. Are you saying that the Department of Veterans Affairs is truly a "totally failed system"? Do you mind elaborating on that? I know they have problems, but I want to learn why you think it's a totally failed system. *(Clarification)*

Ron: Well, let's take mental health disorders. ProPublica's review since 2020 found that the VA's health care network has very serious flaws when it comes to treating veterans with mental illness. I believe this report was based on over 150 investigations and facility surveys.

Bill: Can you tell me more? *(Probe)* Can you send me a link to this review? I've never heard of it and want to see if it's credible. *(Information-Giving)*

Ron: I remember reading there were a lot of problems. I can't remember them all, but I remember missed screenings and staffing shortages.

Bill: Who exactly is ProPublica? *(Clarification)*

Ron: Off the top of my head, I can't remember much, but I do remember they're a very good nonprofit organization dedicated to investigative journalism. They're mainly journalists who have won many awards for their investigative work.

Bill: Can you send me a link to your reports? *(Information-Giving)*

Ron: Absolutely! I'll email it to you tonight.

Bill: I'm not trying to trap you here. I know there can be top-quality investigative journalism. Do you know of any reports, perhaps created by independent academics and experts in medicine and health care, that have evaluated the Department of Veterans Affairs? *(Probe and Information-Giving)*

Ron: Maybe, but let me send you the link to ProPublica. I'd like your thoughts.

A Second Hypothetical (Reversed) Example of Using Listening Skills in a Political Conversation

This next hypothetical conversation between Bill and Ron is on the same topic as before, taking place about a week after the one above.

Ron: Hey Bill, I'm curious if you read the ProPublica link I sent you. It occurred to me that I never asked you why you believe in a government-based national health care system. I'd like to hear your thoughts.

Bill: First, thank you for such a good conversation last week and for asking me to share my views. Right at the outset, your example of the Mayo Clinic was a powerful one. I haven't thought much about the role of nonprofit health care in the United States and have always found it troubling that, unlike so many other developed countries, in our country, for-profit health care tries to make money off of people suffering. I find that thought so bizarre—making money off of people who are suffering, for example, with cancer. I realized this last week, as I looked into it more, that nonprofit health care, like the Mayo Clinic, doesn't make money off of other people's suffering. Instead, money goes into improving services. I can't thank you enough for bringing this to my awareness. The Mayo Clinic has been ranked as the best health care system in the United States for over twenty years!

Ron: I'm glad I said something wise!

Bill: I did look at the ProPublica link and can share my thoughts in a minute, but I'd first like to answer your question about why I believe in government-based health care. My reason is different from yours. My support for government-based national health care rests on saving a huge amount of money from insurance premiums and taxes from preventive services, and I think it's a more Christlike concept.

Ron: Tell me more. *(Probe)*

Bill: If I remember what you shared last week, Ron, you believe that offering free health care will cause abuse because people will be going to doctors for every little thing. What you see as abuse and not being self-reliant, I see as prevention, and being preventive is an act of self-reliance that can save all of us from paying more taxes or insurance premiums.

Ron: I'm interested—tell me more. *(Probe)*

Bill: Preventive care saves money in health care by reducing the cost of treating illnesses and diseases that are caught early. Early detection through regular screenings and checkups can help identify health issues before they become more advanced and expensive. It can also reduce the need for costly hospitalizations and treatments later on. According to the National Institutes of Health, preventive health care services save $7 billion a year, which you and I pay for either in taxes or through our health care insurance. And according to the American Public Health Association, every dollar spent on prevention saves us over $5 in health care spending. Prevention is four times more cost-effective than treatment.

Ron: Let me make sure I understand. The main reason you believe Americans should have a robust national health care system is that it'll save us all money, mainly through prevention. I can't recall the different agencies you just referenced, but I can recall that you just shared that every dollar spent on prevention saves us over five dollars in health care spending. Do I have this right? *(Paraphrase)*

Bill: Yes!

Ron: As you asked last week, could you share links to these two agencies you referenced? I'd like to read those reports myself. *(Information-Giving)*

Bill: Sure, I can send them to you right after we talk.

Ron: How do you see prevention connected to self-reliance? *(Clarification)*

Bill: Prevention is what gives us freedom and choices. If self-reliance is the ability, commitment, and effort to provide life's spiritual and temporal necessities for self and family, having health care enables us to become independent and helps us manage the temporal necessities of life. National health care provides greater freedom and choices through prevention for all people, especially those living in poverty. Self-care is caring for oneself to achieve and maintain good health. It's an active process that involves awareness, self-control, and self-reliance.

Ron: This is fascinating, and I can hear your passion in your voice. *(Reflection)* I see how we both understand self-reliance in different but similar ways. We both see it as connected to independence, managing our own lives, and choice. But I see national health care as creating dependency and wasteful services, whereas you see it as a launching pad for becoming independent, as someone having greater choice to manage their lives, and as a way of acting in self-control. As you shared earlier, you also see prevention through government-based national health care as saving a high degree of money through taxes or insurance premiums. ***(Summarization)***

Bill: You got it! I believe we see the application of self-reliance in different ways. I can also see your concern, Ron, with waste, and there will be some waste, absolutely. Some people will abuse the system, go to doctors needlessly, and waste their money. *(Paraphrase)* Still, I think the greater good is that it will allow people to manage their health care better and prevent so much waste and expense later. It saves way more money treating cancer in stage one through prevention screenings than giving heavy-duty treatment in stage four. It saves money to treat a twelve-year-old with mental health struggles rather than waiting until they're in their forties, living homeless with schizophrenia, and then using so many resources. And let's not forget, it can also prevent early death. I believe this kind of system fosters self-reliance and helps people become independent.

Ron: You shared earlier that you felt government-run national health care is more Christlike. Can you elaborate? *(Clarification)*

Bill: As you know, Mosiah 2:17 in the Book of Mormon tells us that when we're in the service of our fellow beings, we're in the service of our God. In the Bible, Galatians 5:13 is to the point: "By love, serve one another." Government-run national health care will increase taxes, but if you look at the big picture, we save money in the long run. But still, I don't mind paying more taxes for other people to have good health care and can use it to prevent more significant problems and costs. I see it as serving others and helping them get on the path of self-reliance, especially for those struggling in life who are trying to dig themselves out of a hole. With that said, I don't want the government to use the people's money for other sorts of things, such as to pay off university student debt, but for primary health care, it's an act of giving.

Ron: Thanks for sharing. So returning to one of my first questions, did you read the ProPublica link I sent you?

Bill: I did. And in the most respectful way, Ron, I didn't find it convincing. The report stated that ProPublica reviewed many published VA inspectors' general accounts over many years, including 160 surveys and 150 investigations, but, unless I missed it, it didn't provide any links to the primary sources. *(Confrontation)* It only offered a link to one VA inspector's general report that looked at a single patient who died by suicide at the John Cochran division of the VA St. Louis Health Care System in Missouri. Now, I will say that this single report was powerful, but it was just one person at one VA hospital. Do you know how to retrieve more of their references and primary sources? *(Information-Giving)*

Bill: Let me look into it—I thought it provided all the sources.

Conclusion

Listening is a skill set that can be learned, similar to a skill set that must be mastered before playing a sport. As I shared earlier in the chapter, to play basketball, a person would need to learn these skills: dribbling, shooting, passing, rebounding, jumping, footwork, and defense. Likewise, to listen, a person needs to learn these action skills: paraphrasing, clarifying, reflecting, summarizing, probing, information-giving, interpretation, and confrontation.

The two hypothetical examples above are what I hope can happen between people who have different political views. In fact, a good portion of the two examples are based on past good conversations I've had with a handful of different people, as I have often been asked to share my views on Canadian health care with my American friends and have been asked to share my views on American health care to my Canadian friends. (I am both an American citizen and a Canadian citizen and have lived in Canada for approximately twenty-seven years and in the United States for twenty-eight.)

Listening to understand begins with a mindset that was explained in the previous chapter. Listening to understand is based on strong-sense critical/reflective thinking that uses curiosity, listening, and thinking skills to learn and understand other viewpoints and to have insights into our own (not others') cognitive and affective processes. As numerous historians have articulated, part of what made George Washington the greatest American president was his cognitive elasticity and ability to listen. Washington was the "listener in chief." President Russell M. Nelson, our beloved prophet, is another great example of listening, encouraging us to "listen to learn" and following that same counsel himself.

4
Media Literacy to Become Informed in Politics

I WANT TO TELL YOU ABOUT A TIME I WAS HOODWINKED BY MASS MEdia—well before social media had become commonplace—with streaming platforms and podcasts. (Later in the chapter, I differentiate between mass media and social media.)

Shortly after Ricki and I moved to Iowa, a TV commercial showed skiing and snow tubing in an outdoor recreation area a little over an hour away from where we lived. It showed a family just like mine—a husband and wife with young children—having the time of their lives snow tubing, and I imagined having this same type of fun with my good wife and our three young sons. I checked in with Ricki, and we planned a day trip to go.

Unfortunately, it was not even close to my imagined family trip when we arrived. First, the tubing hill was much steeper and faster than I had imagined, and I was surprised at how icy and fast the lanes were. As our two younger sons watched other people speed down the hill, they began to be afraid. This was very unlike the commercial I saw, which showed younger children snow tubing. Still, I had hoped that if our two younger sons watched enough, they'd become excited (my feeble attempt at using systematic desensitization to reduce my son's fear of how high and fast the snow tubing lanes were at this recreation site).[104]

Ricki, Chayce (our oldest son), and I decided to go down the snow tubing lanes once each, as I was hoping that role modeling us having fun might change our two sons' fear response. But as I flew down the hill on my tube, I thought, "This is way too fast for Jonas and Zach!" When Ricki was at the top of the tubing hill getting ready to launch, the staff member decided, without asking, to spin her tube, and it was not an enjoyable ride down for her. She didn't appreciate the spinning, and it frightened our two sons even more—they turned to me and said something like "Mom's going to crash!" with a tone of intense worry. Ricki, Chayce, and I agreed this activity was unsuitable for Jonas and Zachary. I had been hoodwinked! The commercial pulled at my identity as a father and my emotions of wanting to have my sons experience something fun. That's how I got hoodwinked!

Although this experience happened over twenty years ago, well before social media had become mainstream, its manipulation of my identity and emotions is no different than the manipulation that happens today on social media related to political engagement and discussion of social issues.

In the 2024 federal election, for example, it is well known that Donald Trump used fight culture and fighting celebrities streaming platforms (e.g., Dana White Ultimate Fighting Championship President; YouTuber-turned-boxer Jake Paul) to influence a subset of young men to vote for him based on nothing more than a love (emotion) for fighting. Many (not all) fight-club social media streaming sites that championed Donald Trump had little policy analysis or comparisons of how to manage, prevent, or remedy social problems like affordable housing or the opioid crisis. Instead, it was social media manipulation based on (fighting) identity and emotion (love of fight culture), where entertainment was primary (e.g., yelling, shaming of particular political candidates, crude commentary) with scant

---

104. Systematic desensitization is a behavioral therapy intervention that can help reduce anxiety and change reactions to feared situations.

political thought. (I want to add that this is a subset of young men; another subgroup of young men who voted for Trump did so for well-thought-out reasons, such as wanting the economy to improve so they could afford to purchase a house and make a living wage.)

On the other side of the political aisle, celebrity Lady Gaga used Instagram, a social networking platform for sharing photos and videos, to help Kamala Harris during the 2024 federal election, with scant depth of thought. It was no different than the Ultimate Fighting Championship rhetoric for Donald Trump, as it was also about emotion and identity and not much else. The following quotation from a *Daily Beast* article—written by a Kamala Harris staffer who was furious after Harris's positive post-election call-in meeting with staffers—underscores the extent of manipulation: "[Harris's post-election call-in] was detached from the reality of what happened. . . . We are told the fate of democracy is at stake, and then the message is, 'We'll get them next time.'"[105] This upset staffer, who was tricked into falsely believing that the fate of democracy was at stake during the 2024 federal election, is now grappling with the idea that democracy will not be crashing and that it's time to think about the next election in four years. This is no different than the subset of young men not realizing they were being tricked by the Donald Trump team through the fighting culture. Hoodwinked!

Marketing strives to get people interested in a product, often by promoting its offerings so that customers perceive them as desirable, such as celebrities making either Donald Trump or Kamala Harris look and seem cool. Rhona Jackson, program leader for media studies at the University of Derby in the United Kingdom, shared how she was deceived by the media when she went on her first trip to the United States from Britain. Jackson shares the following about her much-anticipated visit to the famous Chinese Theatre tourism site in the Los Angeles area:

---

105. David Gardner, "Harris Staffers Furious over Post-Election Pep Talk: 'Detached from Reality,"' *Daily Beast*, Nov. 8, 2024, https://www.thedailybeast.com/kamala-harris-staffers-furious-over-post-election-pep-talk-detached-from-reality/.

> Visiting the Chinese Theatre brought the realization that whenever this location is filmed, for instance, in the past, for the Oscars Ceremony, we see the stars, the red carpet, and the adoring crowd. Yet, immediately adjacent was wasteland, fronted by old railings sporting tacky advertisements, a bleak contrast to the TV-transmitted glitzy glamour. Media selection and editing conventions ensure that this image never reaches our screens. . . . We made sense of most places by comparing them to screen images, being surprised at our own naivety, having failed to appreciate how extensive our imaginations had been fueled by the metaphoric construction of ideas and desires [based on the media].[106]

At the end of Jackson's narrative, she remarked that her motivation to visit Los Angeles was due to the pleasure she felt from false media marketing, with scant attention toward her own media literacy.

Although many Americans believe that media does not influence them, studies from marketing psychology clearly show how easy it is to be duped by media. Why do you think companies spend enormous amounts of money on media marketing? A minimum advertising budget for sponsoring the *Joe Rogan Experience* podcast is $120,000,[107] and *Fortune* recently reported that the multi-year deal that Spotify signed with that podcast is estimated to be worth up to $250 million.[108] In 2023, according to Statista, the cost for a thirty-second commercial during the NFL Super Bowl was $7 million.[109] Would companies or sponsors pay this much for advertising on *The Joe Rogan*

---

106. Rhona Jackson, "Converging Cultures, Converging Gazes, Contextualizing Perspectives," in *The Media and the Tourist Imagination*, ed. David Crouch, Rhona Jackson, and Felix Thompson (Routledge, 2005), 186.
107. See "Joe Rogan Sponsors," RadioActiveMedia Marketing & Advertising, accessed Feb. 3, 2025, https://radioactivemedia.com/joe-rogan-sponsors/.
108. "Spotify Signs Reported $250M Joe Rogan Deal Two Years After CEO Denounced Podcast Host's Racist Language but Added, 'I Do Not Believe That Silencing Joe Is the Answer,'" *The Associated Press*, Feb. 3, 2024, https://fortune.com/2024/02/03/spotify-joe-rogan-youtube-apple-podcasts/. Spotify is a Swedish audio streaming and media service provider founded in 2006 by Daniel Ek and Martin Lorentzon.
109. Statista is a global data and business intelligence platform. See their report at https://www.statista.com/statistics/217134/total-advertisement-revenue-of-super-bowls/.

Experience or the NFL Super Bowl if persuasion or manipulation of the viewers didn't work? Although, as humans, we want to think we are not fooled or influenced by media, it is better to realize how easily we're deceived and tricked. That's why I began this chapter by sharing how a simple commercial duped me.

One of my favorite media literacy professors, Dr. W. James Potter from UC Santa Barbara, outlined how most Americans are unaware of how much media influences and controls them and that "the more you are aware of how the mass media operate and how they affect you, the more you gain control over those effects, and the more you will distinguish yourself from typical media users who have turned over a great deal of their lives to the mass media without realizing it."[110]

Potter says that when we're not consciously paying attention and carefully evaluating our media exposure, media continually reinforces certain behavioral patterns of exposure until they become automatic habits (e.g., voting for someone based on a love of fight culture or a love of a music genre). Media is a powerful societal force that greatly influences all of us in many areas, including political events and views.

Media and Becoming Informed About Politics

Recent Pew Research Center studies demonstrate the media's influence on how people think and engage in social and political issues and events. A Pew Research study released on November 18, 2024, two weeks after the 2024 federal election, indicates these four key findings:[111]

---

110. W. James Potter, *Media Literacy* (Sage, 2021), xix.
111. See "America's News Influencers," Pew Research Center, Nov. 18, 2024, https://www.pewresearch.org/journalism/2024/11/18/americas-news-influencers/. In this study, "news influencers" refer to individuals who regularly post about current events and civic issues on social media and have at least 100,000 followers on Facebook, Instagram, TikTok, X, or YouTube. News influencers can be journalists who are or were affiliated with a news organization or independent content creators, but they must be people and not organizations.

- About one in five Americans—including a much higher share of adults under thirty (37 percent)—say they regularly get news from social media influencers.
- News influencers are most likely to be found on the social media site X (formerly Twitter), where 85 percent have a presence. However, many are also on other social media sites, such as Instagram (where 50 percent have an account) and YouTube (44 percent).
- Slightly more news influencers explicitly identify as Republican, conservative, or pro–Donald Trump (27 percent of news influencers) than Democratic, liberal, or pro–Kamala Harris (21 percent).
- A clear majority of news influencers are men (63 percent).

A Pew Research study released on July 24, 2024, indicates that 66 percent of US adults use local news outlets, and 54 percent report using social media sites to become informed about political events, such as in deciding on who to vote for.[112] The only source that is higher than news and social media in political decision-making is talking to friends, family members, and neighbors, which is reported at 70 percent. (One possible troubling aspect of chatting with friends, family, and neighbors is if they hold similar values and political views.)

Also reported in the July study is that 59 percent of US adults say it's easy to find the information they need for presidential elections, a statistic I find concerning for two reasons. First, it takes time and energy to understand social and economic problems and how different approaches taken by various political parties might have different benefits. Trying to understand how a Republican or Democratic candidate might deal with the opioid or mental health crisis or precision agriculture takes time. Second, I believe that relying on media—whether mass or social—is a poor way to make political decisions, especially today when it is so straightforward to find one's political tribal group via social media, which then creates a social media echo

---

112. "How Americans Get Local Political News," Pew Research Center, July 24, 2024, https://www.pewresearch.org/journalism/2024/07/24/how-americans-get-local-political-news/.

chamber. This echo chamber delivers a biased, fitted media experience that eliminates opposing viewpoints and differing voices. With the development of social media algorithms, people often only view media that fits their preferences, and then such people are in a comfortable, self-confirming feedback loop. If someone leans right politically, their echo chamber might include social media algorithms linked to these strongly right-leaning media sources: *The Joe Rogan Experience, The Glenn Beck Program Podcast, Fox News,* and the *National Review.* If they're on the left, their echo chamber might include these strongly left-leaning media sources: the *Pod Save America* podcast, *The Michael Moore Podcast, MSNBC,* and the *New Yorker.*

Democracy expects us to learn about events in our nation (or state or cities) by learning about and considering different policy ideas to remedy or prevent social problems and help with community and human flourishing. The actions of (1) becoming informed about social and political issues and (2) engaging in the political process—which are clearly outlined in the "Political Neutrality and Participation"[113] statement by The Church of Jesus Christ of Latter-day Saints—should have members engage in much more than relying on a one-sided social media echo chamber.

I have always found it challenging to locate information for presidential elections and have found that it takes a good amount of time and thinking. But before sharing the things I've learned over the years about developing media literacy skills, I want to share some guidance from Latter-day Saint leaders and General Authorities on the subject of social media.

Counsel from Latter-day Saint Leaders About Social Media

When I summarize what Church leaders and General Authorities counsel regarding social media, I hear the potential for both good and bad. Social media can be used in the Lord's way to communicate

---

113. "Political Neutrality and Participation," The Church of Jesus Christ of Latter-day Saints, June 1, 2023, https://newsroom.churchofjesuschrist.org/official-statement/political-neutrality.

and share goodness. But when used unbecomingly, with simplicity or overuse, it can be harmful or even dangerous.

Regarding overuse, many studies suggest that the average American spends more than seven hours a day on social media, and such high amounts of time on our phones and computer screens scrolling social media has led to sleep deprivation, attention fragmentation, addiction, lack of healthy relationships, and an increase in many mental health disorders (e.g., anxiety, ADHD, depression).[114]

One of the best talks I've heard about social media is from Elder Gary E. Stevenson,[115] where he begins his talk by highlighting how social media can aid in the spreading of "the knowledge of a Savior . . . throughout every nation, kindred, tongue, and people" (Mosiah 3:20) and then identifies Church websites like ChurchofJesusChrist.org (formerly LDS.org and Mormon.org) and mobile apps such as "Gospel Library, Mormon Channel, LDS Tools, and Family Tree." Elder Stevenson then compares the risks connected with social media to a spiritual eclipse that can block the brightness and warmth of the gospel. He states:

> The use of social media, mobile apps, and games can be inordinately time-consuming and can reduce face-to-face interaction. This loss of personal conversation can affect marriages, take the place of valuable spiritual practices, and stifle the development of social skills, especially among youth.
>
> Two additional risks related to social media are idealized reality and debilitating comparisons.

---

114. See Jonathan Haidt, *The Anxious Generation: How the Great Rewiring of Childhood Is Causing an Epidemic of Mental Illness* (Penguin Press, 2024). Haidt's book provides conclusive evidence that mental health disorders began to increase significantly as smartphones and social media became popular around 2010–2015. Haidt argues, persuasively, that social media and smartphones are not just a correlation; it is causing an epidemic of mental health disorders. As a licensed mental health counselor and a professor who has studied mental health for over thirty years, I think Haidt's book is outstanding and a must-read to understand how the social media smartphone nexus has devastating effects on mental health.

115. Gary E. Stevenson, "Spiritual Eclipse," *Ensign* or *Liahona*, Nov. 2017, 46.

> Many (if not most) of the pictures posted on social media tend to portray life at its very best—often unrealistically. We have all seen beautiful images of home decor, wonderful vacation spots, smiling selfies, elaborate food preparation, and seemingly unattainable body images. . . .
>
> Comparing our own seemingly average existence with others' well-edited, perfectly crafted lives as represented on social media may leave us with feelings of discouragement, envy, and even failure.[116]

Idealized reality and debilitating comparisons, what Elder Stevenson refers to as additional risks, are the cognitive distortions of black-or-white thinking, overgeneralization, and jumping to conclusions, which were explained in chapter 2. (In that chapter, I only wrote about cognitive distortions linked to politics, but idealized reality and debilitating comparisons are cognitive distortions located in the profession of mental health counseling and are at the foundation of mood disorders.)

In his closing remarks during the October 2021 general conference, President Nelson stated, "If most of the information you get comes from social or other media, your ability to hear the whisperings of the Spirit will be diminished."[117] And in 2015, Elder David A. Bednar stated this regarding social media:

> Too much time can be wasted, too many relationships can be harmed or destroyed, and precious patterns of righteousness can be disrupted when technology is used improperly. We should not allow even good applications of social media to overrule the better and best uses of our time, energy, and resources. . . . We need not become social media experts or fanatics. And we do not need to spend inordinate amounts of time creating and disseminating elaborate messages.[118]

---

116. Gary E. Stevenson, "Spiritual Eclipse," 46.
117. Russell M. Nelson, "Make Time for the Lord," *Ensign* or *Liahona*, Nov. 2021, 120.
118. David A. Bednar, "Apostle Offers Counsel about Social Media," *Ensign*, Jan. 2015, 17.

President Bonnie L. Oscarson, while serving as Young Women General President, stated this in 2017:

> We live in a culture where more and more we are focused on the small, little screen in our hands than we are on the people around us. We have substituted texting and tweeting for actually looking someone in the eye and smiling or, even rarer, having a face-to-face conversation. We are often more concerned with how many followers and likes we have than with putting an arm around a friend and showing love, concern, and tangible interest. . . . If we are not vigilant in how we use our personal devices, we too can begin to turn inward and forget that the essence of living the gospel is service.[119]

Although social media can be a good communication tool for spreading the gospel, it can certainly harm us by allowing us to make unrealistic and unhealthy comparisons, lowering our ability to hear the whisperings of the Spirit and harming relationships and face-to-face conversations. It also harms how we think about current events, politics, and civic issues.

A Quick History of Media, Mass Media, and Social Media[120]

The following explanations are important to know when it comes to different types of media:

- *Media*, which aims to educate, inform, or entertain, refers to the tools and outlets used to store and deliver information to many people.
- *Mass media* refers to traditional one-directional forms of communication (e.g., television, radio, newspapers) that disseminate information to a large, passive audience.
- *Social media* involves interactive online platforms where users create and share content, actively engaging with each other

---

119. Bonnie L. Oscarson, "The Needs before Us," *Ensign* or *Liahona*, Nov. 2017, 25.
120. This section is based on Keith A. Quesenberry, *Social Media Strategy: Marketing, Advertising, and Public Relations in the Consumer Revolution* (Rowman & Littlefield, 2025), 7–27.

and contributing to conversations (e.g., Facebook, X [formerly Twitter], Instagram, YouTube).

That is, whereas mass media is one-way communication, social media is a two-way dialogue.

Media Literacy[121]

Media literacy education began to be introduced in the United States in the second half of the twentieth century to protect children from the disturbing influences of Hollywood by teaching them to understand how the cinema worked.[122] Media literacy is defined as providing tools to help people reflect, analyze, and interpret the meaning of media messages they encounter. Many studies demonstrate that media literacy can improve social relationships and well-being, reduce susceptibility to misinformation, and aid in the ability to navigate online communities more effectively.[123] In 2022, Kristoffer Boyle, associate professor of communication at Brigham Young University, published an article on the website of The Church of Jesus Christ of Latter-day Saints advocating media literacy to find truth in the misinformation age. Boyle's five media literacy ideas are as follows:

- Rely on multiple sources from different channels and do not rely on one single media source. This includes books, newspaper articles, academic studies, and trusted experts.
- Take time to verify information shared with you, including information cited in media.

---

121. Unless otherwise referenced, this section is based on W. James Potter, *Media Literacy* (Sage, 2021), 1–31.
122. Renee Hobbs and Amy Jensen, "The Past, Present, and Future of Media Literacy Education," *Journal of Media Literacy Education* 1, no. 1 (2009): 1–11.
123. There are scores of studies demonstrating the benefits of media literacy education. In an academic book I authored over ten years ago, I listed over twenty studies, including large-scale experimental design studies, meta-analyses, case studies, and qualitative approaches. That book is titled *Leisure Education: A Person-Centered, System-Directed, Social Policy Perspective*.

- Be aware of and avoid social media echo chambers where our beliefs and opinions are magnified and we are fed information focused solely on our interests.
- Listen to the Spirit and use the Spirit to identify accurate and valuable information.
- Follow the prophet.[124]

Media literacy often includes helping people break down a media message into meaningful elements—creating a brief, clear, and accurate description capturing the essence of a media message—and then comparing the media message to standards, such as the standards of real everyday life or values held by the Church. As an example, with the help of media literacy, a young man or woman may learn that the intended message of a beer advertisement on social media is to project a fake message that men who drink a specific type of beer have attractive women hanging around them and are always having a good time. Evaluating that and comparing it to real life will often showcase the falseness of the advertisement (e.g., young men who drink beer usually do not have attractive women hanging around them, and such a media message is a ploy to exploit young men for profit). In addition, media literacy might have youth learn that 32 percent of all traffic crash fatalities in the United States involve drunk drivers and that in 2022, approximately 13,524 people were killed in alcohol-impaired driving traffic deaths (all, of course, preventable deaths).[125]

Think back to the counsel of Elder Stevenson where he talks about the additional risk of debilitating comparisons that occur via social media and states, "Many (if not most) of the pictures posted on social media tend to portray life at its very best—often unrealistically. We have all seen beautiful images of home decor, wonderful vacation spots, smiling selfies, elaborate food preparation, and seemingly unattainable body images. . . . Comparing our own seemingly average existence with others' well-edited, perfectly crafted lives as represented

---

124. Kristoffer Boyle, "Finding Truth in the Misinformation Age," *Liahona*, Oct. 2022.

125. "Drunk Driving," National Highway Traffic Safety Administration, accessed Feb. 4, 2025, https://www.nhtsa.gov/risky-driving/drunk-driving.

on social media may leave us with feelings of discouragement, envy, and even failure."[126]

Although Elder Stevenson is not associating his talk with media literacy education—instead, he is speaking the words that he feels have been prompted by the Spirit—he is engaging in media literacy education principles by breaking down a message and then evaluating the media message to the standards of real, everyday life (e.g., elaborate food preparation, unattainable body images).

Actions You Can Take Against the Onslaught of Mass Media and Social Media

Before I provide action steps that you can take to become informed so that you can engage in the political process during this era of so much political deception, I have one simple message: *It takes a large amount of time to become politically knowledgeable and well-versed.* It is more complex than just watching the news or your favorite (often confirmation-biased) podcasts or talking with a few family members or friends (ones who usually have similar political views). Rather, being informed about politics is a lifelong learning pursuit. I personally dedicate a few hours a week to this sacred obligation. Democracy demands that of me.

When Joseph Smith received a revelation in December 1832 to establish a school for the elders of the Church in Kirtland (the School of the Prophets), it offered both spiritual and secular instruction involving these nonspiritual topics: current events, history, reading, writing, and mathematics. Based on Doctrine and Covenants 88:78–80, this school specifically instructed Church members to understand better the "perplexities of the nations" and "a knowledge also of countries and of kingdoms."[127] The Church of Jesus Christ of Latter-day Saints views secular learning as a paramount element of wisdom. President Russell M. Nelson stated that obtaining an education is a religious responsibility because of the sacred regard for each person's intellect.[128]

---

126. Gary E. Stevenson, "Spiritual Eclipse," 46.
127. Church History Topic, "School of the Prophets," Gospel Library.
128. Russell M. Nelson, "Where Is Wisdom?," *Ensign*, Nov. 1992, 6.

It is a religious responsibility that takes more effort, time, and thought than being entertained by a podcast. Again, *it takes a good amount of time to become politically knowledgeable and well-versed.*

With that in mind, let's look at five specific steps you can take to become politically informed.

Action 1: Genuinely Listen to the Opposing Candidate

First, you can listen, without interruption, to the political candidate you oppose with respect, dignity, and an open mind. That is, hear both or multiple sides.

In chapter 1, I outlined six core political cognitive distortions, and identifying them in your thinking is vital to this action step. In chapter 2, I outlined the actions of listening. Both cognitive self-awareness and listening are needed for this action step, in order to hear the thoughts of the political candidate that you oppose or have serious questions about.

To this end, I often think of the people (everyday citizens and state legislature)[129] who attended the 1858 Lincoln–Douglas debates. The Lincoln–Douglas debates consisted of seven different debates as they were competing for the United States Senate seat in Illinois. Most important to this chapter, each debate lasted three hours—a good amount of time dedicated to hearing a person without interruptions—and attendees were forced to listen to both sides. In each debate, Douglas or Lincoln would open with an hour-long speech, and then the other would speak for ninety minutes. The first speaker then had thirty minutes to share a rebuttal. (In the seven debates, Douglas, as the incumbent, was allowed to go first four times.)[130]

This is so very different from today's presidential debates in which media moderators give candidates a few minutes to answer a question

---

129. Until the Seventeenth Amendment was ratified to the United States Constitution in 1913, senators were elected by their respective state legislatures.

130. Doris Kearns Goodwin, *Team of Rivals: The Political Genius of Abraham Lincoln* (Simon & Schuster, 2006), 200–208. See also "The Lincoln-Douglas Debates of 1858," Lincoln Home National Historic Site, accessed Feb. 4, 2025, https://home.nps.gov/liho/learn/historyculture/debates.htm.

and are constantly changing topics. Today's presidential debates align with a population that seems to have an inattention problem, cannot listen for more than a few minutes, and seems to need the topic changed often. Today's presidential debates, and then follow-up analysis, are entertainment-oriented, such as podcast influencers yelling and using violent, crude, and shaming rhetoric. Such a lack of depth and breadth. Such a lack of respect. Imagine being at one of the Lincoln–Douglas debates, and imagine you were a Lincoln supporter. At the debate you attended, you had to hear Douglas speak first and listen for an hour. Then you could hear Lincoln speak for ninety minutes, and then you needed to listen to Douglas a second time share a rebuttal and concluding thoughts for another half hour.[131] In addition, there was no immediate political analysis or spin by right- or left-leaning media within seconds after a debate. Those who attended could immediately reflect on what they had just heard, and a few days later, analysis or spin happened via left- and right-leaning newspapers.

This older format is much better because it requires people to sustain attention for three hours and hear both sides, where both speakers have ample time to speak. That is, it allows depth and breadth in political thought, including hearing the views of the candidate you oppose. Then you could reflect on it *before* hearing the analysis.

In the modern world, too many Americans become informed by clicking on sites that already align with their political values and listening to summaries that make the opposite candidate sound like a fool through media manipulation. Too many Americans want entertainment as they engage in politics instead of training their minds to be disciplined. Too many Americans want to be a live spectator at a presidential debate so they can cheer their candidate, boo the other, and experience emotional fireworks (emotions based on conflict) rather than hear both and be engaged in a sacred and reflective process. Few Americans will go—with an open mind—and hear a candidate they oppose in order to learn and become more informed. Few Americans take the time it requires to become knowledgeable and well-versed.

---

131. In addition, it is well known that people across the Midwest traveled in droves to see Lincoln and Douglas speak, and travel could take hours or even days.

Almost thirty-five years ago, internationally known sociologist Robert Bellah (and his colleagues) stated, "The public votes (when it votes) largely for political personalities as they display themselves through managed, handled, and 'massaged' campaign appearances and the thirty-second 'image bytes.' . . . It is no wonder that Americans feel disaffected from politics."[132] Bellah added that the eighteenth-century idea of the public was not just a conglomeration of interest groups but a discursive community capable of thinking with depth and breadth about the common good. He adds that political debates today (remember, he wrote this in 1991) have become "expensive media wars with little sustained intellectual content"[133] and how paramount it is that people in the modern world take time in their lives to understand and study political topics. He states, "Democracy means paying attention."[134]

Unlike the 1858 Lincoln–Douglas debate, today we do not have to travel for hours or days to attend an event. Instead, we can watch candidates' entire speeches and rallies—including those of the political candidate you oppose—from our smartphones and computers. This is where we can use internet technologies to hear the other side. This is more respectful and intellectual than watching short sound bites from social media clips and entertainment-based podcasts affirming our political views (i.e., the echo chamber).

Action 2: Read Books by Political Candidates

Second, you can read books written by candidates (and their core supporters) and on specific political ideas and concepts.

In many ways, this action step is a continuation of the first action step because reading a book that political candidates have written is a way of hearing their voices without interruption. Most candidates who run for president have written books. In the last federal election,

---

132. Robert N. Bellah, Richard Madsen, Steven M. Tipton, William M. Sullivan, and Ann Swidler, *The Good Society* (Knopf Doubleday Publishing Group, 1992), 133

133. Bellah et al., *The Good Society*, 142.

134. Bellah et al., *The Good Society*, 254.

Kamala Harris wrote *The Truths We Hold: An American Journey*, and Donald Trump wrote *The Art of the Deal* and *Crippled America: How to Make America Great Again*. Reading their books is an excellent way to better understand their thoughts and allow them to share those thoughts holistically.

Although many people think of reading as a leisure activity, I view it as a condition, and even a requirement, of democratic life. That's because it helps people understand a topic with greater depth, breadth, clarity, precision, and accuracy. It also helps people see the relevance of a political subject to everyday life. While frequently credited to Thomas Jefferson, the phrase "an educated citizenry is a vital requisite for our survival as a free people" is a spurious quote (that is, it cannot be found in any of Jefferson's documented writings), it does correctly reflect his paramount belief in the vivacity of an educated populace for a healthy democracy.[135] (And I want to make it clear that an educated populace does not mean having degrees; instead, it means studying a topic with depth, breadth, and precision.)

Perhaps this is why historians have noted that Abraham Lincoln was known as always carrying a book and was often observed reading whenever he had free time.[136] Likewise, although George Washington was not as ubiquitous of a reader when compared to other Founding Fathers—such as John Adams, Thomas Jefferson, Benjamin Franklin, Alexander Hamilton, or James Madison—award-winning Washington biographer Ron Chernow underscores that General George Washington had thousands of books in his study and that

---

135. See "An educated citizenry is a vital requisite for our survival as a free people (Spurious Quotation)," The Jefferson Monticello, accessed Feb. 4, 2025, https://www.monticello.org/research-education/thomas-jefferson-encyclopedia/educated-citizenry-vital-requisite-our-survival-free-people-spurious/. See also "An Educated Citizenry," Professional Educators of Tennessee, Apr. 13, 2023, https://www.proedtn.org/news/637495/An-Educated-Citizenry.htm.
136. Goodwin, *Team of Rivals*, 52.

he was "a far more voracious reader than generally recognized."[137] Chernow goes on to say, "For [Washington's] eclectic postwar readings, he had lined up Voltaire's *Letters to Several Friends*, John Locke's *An Essay Concerning Human Understanding*, and Gibbon's *The History of the Decline and Fall of the Roman Empire*. Showing a decided biographical bent, he ordered the lives of Charles XII of Sweden, Louis XV of France, and Peter the Great of Russia."[138]

In his role as president of the Constitutional Convention, Washington had to be nonpartisan and nonspeaking. However, he followed the debates closely and later stated he "read every oral and printed information on both sides of the question that could be procured."[139] Reading and writing are linked, as they are both spaces to reflect and think, which includes thinking about one's own thoughts and about the thoughts that other people offer. Washington's writing can only be described as extraordinary and gigantic, with his literary repository consisting of "thirty and three volumes of copied letters of the General's, besides three volumes of private, seven volumes of general orders, and bundles and bundles of letters to Generals."[140]

I am as busy as the next person, but I still schedule time to read about political and social issues on a weekly basis. A "time substitution" I use so I have time to read is that I engage in almost no social platforms (other than podcasts). I was only involved in Facebook when I opened an account to sell a car five years ago. That's it. I once viewed LinkedIn and accidentally created an account but never posted anything. No Twitter/X or Instagram. I'm not getting lost on my smartphone, reading irrelevant and useless information. No doom scrolling. No reading juicy social gossip. No inordinate amount of time is dedicated to constantly updating my social media profile so

---

137. Ron Chernow, *Washington: A Life* (Penguin Press, 2010), 470. To learn of the extensive daily reading schedules/patterns of many founding fathers, and what books they actually read and found paramount, see Jeffrey Rosen, *The Pursuit of Happiness: How Classical Writers on Virtue Inspired the Lives of the Founders and Defined America* (Simon & Schuster, 2024).

138. Chernow, *Washington: A Life*, 470.

139. Chernow, *Washington: A Life*, 530.

140. Chernow, *Washington: A Life*, 472.

other people know what's going on in my life or so I can brag about myself. I would instead read a book by knowledgeable people about something I find important. Let me provide two personal examples.

LEARNING ABOUT THE US CONSTITUTION

In December of 2022, I became naturalized as a US citizen and pledged my allegiance to the United States flag—a promise of loyalty. This event occurred in a small room at the Neal Smith Federal Building in Des Moines, Iowa. It was a sacred moment. The year prior, I read seven books on American democracy and the US Constitution from distinguished historians and constitutional scholars. During elections and political debates, I constantly hear politicians talking about the Constitution, often accusing the other party of not following or understanding it, so I wanted to learn about the supreme law of the United States that establishes the government's structure and powers and how it protects the rights of citizens.

Of the seven books I read, perhaps the most paramount was *The Words That Made Us: America's Constitutional Conversation, 1760–1840* by Dr. Akhil Reed Amar. The other books I read were *Freedom* by Dr. Annelien de Dijn, *The Broken Constitution: Lincoln, Slavery, and the Refounding of America* by Dr. Noah Feldman, *Team of Rivals: The Political Genius of Abraham Lincoln* by Dr. Doris Kearns, *1776* by David McCullough, and *The Bill of Rights* by Dr. Akhil Amar. That took a lot of time!

This last summer, to better understand how the reconstruction period (1865 to 1877) after the American Civil War transformed the Constitution (with the ratification of the thirteenth, fourteenth, and fifteenth amendments), I read Dr. Eric Foner's two books *The Second Founding: How the Civil War and Reconstruction Remade the Constitution* and *Reconstruction: America's Unfinished Revolution*,

1863–1877.[141] I learned that the thirteenth, fourteenth, and fifteenth amendments safeguarded the Bill of Rights. Lincoln and Congress knew that if states' rights still held greater power than federal rights, most Confederate states would return to slavery and refuse to grant equal rights to all people. The creation of these three amendments—and giving greater power to the federal government—ensured those rights and allowed the Bill of Rights to flourish, thus making democracy genuinely blossom.

Learning About Religious Freedom

During elections and political debates, I continually hear the topic of religious freedom. In the run-up to the 2024 federal election, the *Deseret News*, for example, had many articles on religious freedom.[142] In the last three years, I have read seven books on religious freedom and have become a regular attendee of the Iowa Religious Freedom Day summit, held in Des Moines (and I was a presenter in 2024). On April 13, 2023, I attended the Iowa Religious Freedom Day summit and listened to Dr. G. Marcus Cole, dean of the Notre Dame Law School, speak on the topic. Afterward, in an email, I asked him which two books he would recommend I read to understand religious freedom better. He recommended *The Right to Be Wrong: Ending the Culture War Over Religion in America* by Kevin Seamus Hasson and *The Culture of Disbelief: How American Law and Politics Trivialize Religious Devotion* by Stephen L. Carter. I read both books.

I then asked a trusted colleague of mine at the University of Northern Iowa—who teaches in the religious studies program and has an academic background in religious freedom—what books he suggested I should read. After I asked him, he shared that he needed

---

141. Eric Foner, professor emeritus of history at Columbia University, specializes in the Civil War and reconstruction, slavery, and nineteenth-century America. He has also been the curator of several museum exhibitions, including the prize-winning "A House Divided: America in the Age of Lincoln" at the Chicago Historical Society. His other book, *The Fiery Trial: Abraham Lincoln and American Slavery*, won the Pulitzer Prize for History in 2011.

142. See, for example, Kelsey Dallas, "Trump, Harris and the Future of Religious Freedom," *Deseret News*, Oct 22, 2024, https://www.deseret.com/faith/2024/10/22/kamala-harris-religion-donald-trump/.

to tell me his academic view, which is that religious freedom is more of a myth and that religious freedom has a history of being used by powerful religious groups to dominate minority religious groups. I was excited to read an opposing viewpoint. He suggested I read *The Impossibility of Religious Freedom* by Winnifred Fallers Sullivan and *The Myth of the American Religious Freedoms* by David Sehat. I read both books.

He further shared that he felt that The Church of Jesus Christ of Latter-day Saints was one of the minority religions that has been historically mistreated by dominant and powerful Christian churches and suggested I read *The Mormon Question: Polygamy and the Constitutional Conflict in Nineteenth-Century America* by Sarah Barringer Gordon.[143] So I read that book. I then explored how religious freedom is explained to everyday Christian Americans by reading Ken Starr's *Religious Liberty in Crisis*. To learn more about preserving religious freedom for all—including minority religious groups—I read Thomas Berg's *Religious Liberty in a Polarized Age*.

I have learned so much and am a deep believer in religious freedom. I now feel that I'm in a better position to evaluate politicians who bring up the topic of religious freedom during state and federal elections. In addition, this reading has also helped me understand, with clarity, why people from minority religions believe that religious freedom is more lore (than actual) and are deeply untrusting of its promotion. A good African American friend of mine who serves as a reverend in a predominantly African American church in Iowa has outright told me of her mistrust and frustration with religious

---

143. For an excellent review of Sarah Barringer Gordon's book, see Terry L. Givens, "*The Mormon Question: Polygamy and Constitutional Conflict in Nineteenth-Century America* Sarah Barringer Gordon," *BYU Studies Quarterly* 41, no. 3 (2002): article 9, https://scholarsarchive.byu.edu/byusq/vol41/iss3/9. The best book I have read that has helped me understand the historical practice of polygamy among Latter-Day Saints (1840s until the 1890s) is *Let's Talk about Polygamy* by Brittany Chapman Nash, published by Deseret Book in 2021.

freedom and its history of predominantly white churches using it to harm Black churches and other minority religions.[144]

The two greatest presidents in American history—George Washington and Abraham Lincoln—found time in their busy days to read and reflect. I believe in following their examples in modern times.

Action 3: Rely On Multiple Sources from Different Channels

This action step is word for word what Dr. Kristoffer Boyle stated in his article advocating media literacy on the Church's website.[145] He adds that this includes books, newspaper articles, academic studies, and trusted experts. Boyle suggests not relying on one single media source.

AllSides is a public benefit corporation that identifies media sources with an extreme left, moderate left, center, moderate right, and extreme right viewpoint.[146] Extreme right sources that will slant political and social issues exceptionally to the right (conservative perspective) include *The American Conservative, Brietbart, Federalists, Fox News, National Review, Newsmax,* and *The New York Post.* Moderate right sources that will pitch political and social issues relatively to the right (conservative perspective) include *Dispatch, Fox Business, Just the News, The Wall Street Journal, Washington Examiner,* and *The Washington Times.* Extreme left sources that will push political and social issues superbly to the left (liberal perspective) include *The Atlantic, The Daily Beast, Mother Jones, MSNBC, The New Yorker,* and *Slate.* Moderate left sources that will pitch political and social issues somewhat to the left (liberal perspective) include *ABC News, Bloomberg, CBS News, The New York Times, National Public Radio, Time,* and *The Washington Post.* Center sources that do not have an intentionally

---

144. I also want to share that the past five years, I have served on the Cedar Valley Interfaith Council that serves northeast Iowa. Our meetings have often discussed religious freedom in formal and informal ways.
145. Kristoffer Boyle, "Finding Truth in the Misinformation Age," *Liahona*, Oct. 2022.
146. See https://www.allsides.com/media-bias/media-bias-chart.

left- or right-slanted focus include *BBC News*, *The Christian Science Monitor*, *CNBC*, *Forbes*, *Newsweek*, and *The Hill*.

Related to this third action step—to use multiple sources—one strategy is to read about the news or specific social or political topics from a left, right, and center perspective. That is, if you want to learn about a new cabinet member that the president has chosen, such as secretary of defense or secretary of state, to understand this topic better and the pros and cons of such a candidate, it would be wise to read a left-, right-, and center-leaning article, such as one from *The New York Times* (left), *National Review* (right), and *Newsweek* (center). It's the same if you want to understand the political implications of foreign countries or new domestic policies related to homelessness, immigration, or mental health crises. In most cases (but certainly not all), after reading all these perspectives, I find the truth to be somewhere in the middle.

Perhaps one of the most paramount problems with social media is the fact that it often acts as an echo chamber. As I've mentioned before, this refers to a social media ecosystem in which participants encounter beliefs that enlarge or reinforce their preexisting beliefs. A study a few years ago posited that Americans live in a partisan echo chamber, where voters were 10 to 30 percent less likely to know stories unfavorable to their political party; instead, they consume news that confirms their views. AllSides attempts to combat this by providing news stories on their website from left, center, and right sources.[147] Ground News is another site that allows users to compare media coverage from across the political spectrum, understanding how left, center, and right news sources are covering a political story or issue.[148]

Listening to multiple sources from all sides applies to other media as well, not just social media. An open-minded person could learn about current events and civic issues by going to podcasts like *The Sean Hannity Show* (conservative), *The Rachel Maddow Show* (liberal), and the *Not Another Politics Podcast* (center). When it comes to

---

147. See https://www.allsides.com/media-bias/media-bias-chart.
148. See https://ground.news/.

evaluating web pages and other media sources, including podcasts, the American Library Association (ALA) offers these guidelines:[149]

- **Consider the source:** Consider the author's credibility (how qualified they are to speak on the topic) and the links and sources supporting the article.
- **Check the date:** Each web page should indicate its currency.
- **Consider the purpose:** Consider if the item might be satire or promotional.
- **Check your biases:** Be aware of your own biases.
- **Search other news outlets:** See if other news outlets widely report the news.

The ALA also offers general criteria for evaluating library collections:[150]

- **Currency and timeliness:** How current and timely is the material?
- **Accuracy, quality, and depth:** Evaluate the material's accuracy, quality, and depth.
- **Relevancy:** Consider how relevant the subject or title is to the institution's needs.

Dr. Kristoffer Boyle's article on media literacy also advocates listening to expert opinions and reading academic studies. The dictionary defines an *expert* as "having, involving, or displaying special skill or knowledge derived from training or experience."[151] In regulated professions (e.g., medicine, law, mental health counseling, police, K–12 teaching),[152] that training is communicated by degrees and licensures and, to a lesser degree, certifications based on earning a specific degree from a university or a training school (e.g., law enforcement academy).

---

149. "Resource Guides," American Library Association, accessed Feb. 3, 2025, https://libguides.ala.org/informationevaluation.

150. "Selection Criteria," American Library Association, accessed Feb. 3, 2025, https://www.ala.org/tools/challengesupport/selectionpolicytoolkit/criteria.

151. *Merriam-Webster.com Dictionary*, s.v. "expert," accessed February 3, 2025, https://www.merriam-webster.com/dictionary/expert.

152. In regulated professions, there are laws regulating who can practice.

For example, in Iowa, becoming a professional expert in mental health counseling requires licensure through the Bureau of Professional Licensure and the Board of Behavioral Health Professionals. Becoming a licensed mental health counselor (LMHC) in the Hawkeye State requires earning a master's degree in clinical mental health counseling (from a CACREP-accredited university), passing the National Board for Certified Counselors (NBCC) exam, accruing at least 3,000 supervised counseling experience hours (the equivalent of two years of full-time employment), and then applying for a permanent LMHC license. An LMHC license in Iowa communicates that someone holds professional expertise in the specific area of mental health and mental health counseling (but not in other areas like agriculture or business leadership).

To understand social and political issues related to mental health, there is wisdom in listening to licensed mental health counselors or professional bodies representing such professionals, such as the American Counseling Association or the American Psychological Association. These professional experts and organizations can share expert opinions and relevant research studies related to social and political issues, such as if a mental health support program for farmers in Iowa is a good use of state funds.

In unregulated professions (e.g., biologist, business economist, computer scientist), where there are no laws regulating who can practice, expertise is typically based on degrees, internal training (e.g., apprenticeships), and years of experiences. For example, a diesel or car mechanic can share a high degree of trustworthy information related to the pros and cons of electric and gas engines as it relates to state and government policies.

Becoming an academic expert begins with holding a doctor of philosophy (Ph.D.) but also requires sustained publications in top-notch peer-reviewed journals.[153] Those who are more expert have

---

153. A peer-reviewed journal is a quality control procedure for scholarly research. In short, a manuscript submitted for publication is systematically and rigorously examined and evaluated by peers (other experts in the same field) before being accepted in a journal, ensuring that the quality and accuracy of the research is high and meets demanding and meticulous academic standards.

higher numbers of peer-reviewed publications and citations in top-tier journals and are often distinguished by being selected to join academic or professional societies or receive awards. For example, one distinguished research award in medicine is the Albany Prize in Medicine and Biomedical Research, which provides a $500,000 prize for exceptional work in medicine and biomedical research. This award communicates the highest level of academic (research) knowledge and expertness. Each year, the American Counseling Association (ACA) committee votes on the ACA research award to recognize high-quality, original research conducted by an ACA member. An ACA member who earned a research award is a high-level research expert. Being elected as a fellow in the Academy of Leisure Science or the American Society for Legal History recognizes an academic researcher who has influenced their field of study. Fellowships communicate expert distinction.

Earlier in this chapter, I shared that a year before being naturalized as an American citizen, I had read seven books on American democracy and the US Constitution, all from distinguished historians and constitutional scholars. One was Dr. Akhil Reed Amar, a Sterling Professor of Law and Political Science at Yale University. When you read his university profile,[154] you learn that he has authored over a hundred law articles and several books, and his books have earned various awards, such as the Yale University Press Governors' Award. Dr. Amar's academic labor has secured awards from the American Bar Association and the Federalist Society, and Supreme Court justices have cited him in more than four dozen cases. Dr. Amar regularly testifies before Congress at the invitation of both parties. In addition, he typically ranks among America's five most-cited mid-career legal scholars in surveys of judicial and scholarly citations. This is a high-level academic expert, so I chose to read two books he had authored on the Constitution and the Bill of Rights.

Some people can be both professional *and* academic experts who keep one foot in their professional practice and another in academic writing and research, sometimes called scholar-practitioners or

---

154. See https://law.yale.edu/akhil-reed-amar.

researcher-practitioners. Thomas B. Griffith, who wrote the foreword in this book, is a professional-academic expert. As outlined on his faculty profile at Harvard University,[155] he was appointed to the United States Court of Appeals for the DC Circuit by President George W. Bush in 2005. He retired from the DC Circuit in 2020 and is currently special counsel at the law firm of Hunton Andrews Kurth and a fellow at the Wheatley Institution at Brigham Young University. In 2021, President Joe Biden appointed him to the Presidential Commission on the Supreme Court. He has also published many articles in professional and academic journals.

A 2022 research report that Judge Griffith helped coauthor is an example of how everyday people can read expert opinion and academic studies—again, a suggestion in Dr. Boyle's media literacy article—to become politically knowledgeable and well-versed. This research report was laser-focused on whether there was any truth to the claim that the 2020 election was stolen from Donald Trump and that Joe Biden won due to fraud in the election system, an intense political debate and conversation piece after the 2020 federal election and going into the 2024 election.

In this 72-page report,[156] Judge Griffith enlisted a group of fellow conservatives (which included two former judges, two retired US senators, and a former US solicitor general) to investigate all claims that the 2020 election had been manipulated or stolen, and they spent nine months gathering and analyzing data. For context, as part of Trump's postelection attempts to retain the presidency, he and his supporters filed 64 cases containing 187 counts of election fraud in the six key battleground states. Griffith's report articulates that all 64 cases were refuted and concludes by stating, "Analyses have shown that Trump lost not because of fraud but because a small but significant subset of

---

155. See https://hls.harvard.edu/faculty/thomas-griffith/.

156. John Danforth, Benjamin Ginsberg, Thomas B. Griffith, David Hoppe, J. Michael Luttig, Michael W. McConnell, Theodore B. Olson, Gordon H. Smith, *Lost, Not Stolen The Conservative Case that Trump Lost and Biden Won the 2020 Presidential Election* (2022), https://drive.google.com/file/d/1aqorZ61AYFqZU-EDQBBzjqfvAoC5nKcB/view.

Republican voters supported the GOP's candidates down-ballot but did not vote for Trump."[157]

Relying on multiple and different sources (such as left, right, and center podcasts and news), reading books featuring different political views or on very specific topics (e.g., religious freedom), examining expert opinions and research reports and studies, and hearing the voices of professional people and organizations are all important steps in becoming informed on political and social issues.

ACTION 4: ENGAGE IN LESS ENTERTAINMENT AND MORE DISCIPLINED AND SOMBER REFLECTION

Serious thinking is not about being entertained. And in America, I don't think that the reason we appreciate the Founding Fathers is because they help us laugh. So many of the Founding Fathers were engaged in disciplined and somber reflection as they prepared their thoughts, debates, and dialogues and were concentrated readers. Again, we don't admire them because they entertain us—we appreciate their brilliance, thinking, academic work ethic, pragmatic engagement, and moral character. More Americans need to create a mindset of somber reflection when it comes to political engagement, because becoming responsible, informed citizens—as outlined in the Church's "Political Neutrality and Participation" statement—requires serious, disciplined actions.

Another problem with social media usage for political thinking is that much (though not all) of social media leans heavily towards entertainment as a primary focus. Educational entertainment, sometimes called edutainment, is media designed to educate through entertainment. Over forty years ago, Neil Postman stated in his popular book *Amusing Ourselves to Death* that entertainment-focused thinking about important political and social issues will create a dangerous state of public affairs and discourse. Drawing on and comparing George Orwell's book *1984* with Aldous Huxley's novel *Brave New World*, Postman outlines how dystopia will not come from a dark "Big Brother" force (like in *1984*) but from an entertainment force in

---

157. Danforth et al., *Lost, Not Stolen*, 6.

which people will adore technology that will undo their capacities to think (like in *Brave New World*). The very last sentence of Postman's book is this: "For in the end, [Huxley] was trying to tell us that what afflicted the people in *Brave New World* was not that they were laughing instead of thinking, but that they did not know what they were laughing about and why they had stopped thinking."[158]

Too much media in politics is about being amused and experiencing some feeling state (emotional arousal) through yelling, swearing, crude jokes, and shaming of the opposite candidates or parties. That is, enjoying three left- or right-leaning candidates verbally beating up and even bullying a single person who has a different political view—laughing and cheering at people who mock those with different political views. Too many Americans (though not all) want to attend political debates to see fireworks, not to reflect with depth, and want to boo and hiss at their opponent and cheer for their candidate, much like World Wrestling Entertainment.

Citing research that used neuroscience and fMRI scans to monitor the brain, social and moral psychologist Jonathan Haidt argued that "extreme partisanship may be literally addictive." Viewers who watch more and more fanatical political social media experience an overabundance of dopamine release, resulting in obsessive patterns of behavior.[159]

The key is to dedicate time each day or week to engage in education and somber reflection on various social and political matters, not view politics as just another source of entertainment.

Action 5: Participate in the Social and Political Spheres in the Real World

In many ways, this last suggestion may seem irrelevant to media literacy. After all, engagement in the real world is *not* engagement in the media world, and this chapter is about media literacy. But I am

---

158. Neil Postman, *Amusing Ourselves to Death: Public Discourse in the Age of Show Business* (Penguin Books, 1985), 163.

159. Jonathan Haidt, *The Righteous Mind: Why Good People Are Divided by Politics and Religion* (Vintage, 2012), 103.

suggesting this action because when we participate in the real world, it is often a totally different experience than what we believe the real world is like from engagement with media sources. It's just like the story I shared to begin this chapter, where my imagined view of the outdoor tubing hill was very different than when I was physically present at this tubing hill.

As I have shared elsewhere in this book, a Pew Research study found that 75 percent of Democrats and 64 percent of Republicans believe that those in the other party are more closed-minded than other Americans. In addition, 55 percent of Republicans and 47 percent of Democrats view members of the other party as more immoral than other Americans. Yet a recent opinion piece in *The Seattle Times* tells a different tale of two people with very different political values who see the value in the other from their real-world experience of working together on a county political council in the state of Washington. This shared and coauthored article by Jared Mead (who identifies as a Democrat and serves as chair of the Snohomish County Council) and Nate Nehring (who identifies as a Republican and serves as vice chair of the Snohomish County Council) details their commitment to finding common ground. Their shared opinion piece, with an explicit message of proof that Democrats and Republicans can work together, concludes with this:

> What the two of us learned from participants at the first event was that it is far easier for people to have respectful discussions about politics if we're able to humanize each other despite disagreement and work in good faith to understand differing perspectives. After we all shared a bit about our family histories and where our kids are going to school, it naturally became much more difficult to demonize one another.
>
> That certainly aligns with what we've discovered about our own working relationship; seeing the other person as a human, giving the benefit of the doubt, and being open to honest conversations on tough subjects can go a long way in arriving at common ground. The more we can commit to living out these principles

with our neighbors, the quicker our nation will find healing—one conversation at a time.[160]

For over five years, I have served on the Cedar Valley Interfaith Council in the Cedar Falls / Waterloo area of Iowa. Not only is this council made up of leaders from different religions and faith-based institutions, but it also is made of people who identify as Democrats and Republicans, and we have always worked together. There have been times when I have become frustrated with council members' work and views, and I am sure others have experienced similar frustration with me and others, but we have always worked well together.

One of my favorite people from history is Jane Addams who won worldwide recognition in the first third of the twentieth century as a pioneer social worker in America and as the first American woman to win the Nobel Peace Prize, in 1931.[161] In 1889, she and Ellen Gates Starr leased a large home in one of the poorest districts in Chicago in order to open a center for a higher civic and social life. In the late 1800s, this was known as Hull House, a social settlement house, but today it is often viewed as the beginning of the two professions of social work and community parks and recreation.

What was amazing about Jane Addams is she brought people together from diverse ethnic groups that tended to dislike or hate each other, and together, working as a group for the common good of their neighborhoods, they developed friendships and did so much good in their communities.[162] In my past historical research, I concluded that Jane Addams built the successful Hull House settlement house on contact theory, or the strategy that if positive contact and interaction

---

160. Jared Mead and Nate Nehring, "We Are Proof That Democrats and Republicans Can Work Together," *The Seattle Times*, Feb. 28, 2023, https://www.seattletimes.com/opinion/we-are-proof-that-democrats-and-republicans-can-work-together/.

161. There are many books written about Jane Addams, but my favorite is Jean Bethke Elshtain, *Jane Addams and the Dream of American Democracy* (Basic Books, 2002).

162. The Jane Addams Hull-House created much transformation community change, but to just name a few, her work developed the first public playground, youth groups, and public baths in Chicago, the first factory laws in Illinois, and the first citizenship preparation classes in the United States.

between diverse people occur, then their attitudes toward one another will change in a positive manner.[163] Three conditions that will cause positive attitude change are as follows:

- Contact environments should be based on equal status
- Contact should be personal and persist over time
- Contact results in positive emotion if common goals are established

Kelsey Dallas, reporting for the *Deseret News*, underscores how so many opposition groups came together when President Bill Clinton signed the Religious Freedom Restoration Act in 1993. As Dallas stated:

> The bill, called the Religious Freedom Restoration Act, had come together through the combined efforts of Democrats and Republicans, evangelicals and Muslims, The Church of Jesus Christ of Latter-day Saints and the ACLU, and many, many other groups willing to put aside their political and religious differences to strengthen legal protections for people of faith.
>
> It had been shepherded through the Senate by two legendary leaders of their respective parties: Democratic Sen. Ted Kennedy of Massachusetts and Republican Sen. Orrin Hatch of Utah.
>
> As Clinton prepared to sign the bill into law, he spoke about how it carried forward the Founders' dream of building a pluralistic nation, a place in which religious communities had the right to live according to their beliefs and an important role to play in safeguarding democracy. . . .
>
> In the 30 years since Clinton spoke those words on Nov. 16, 1993, the Religious Freedom Restoration Act has done what its diverse array of supporters hoped it would do. It's enabled people of faith, including members of minority religions, to challenge

---

163. Rodney B. Dieser, "Jane Addams and Hull-House: Understanding the Role of Recreation and Leisure in Bridging Cross-Cultural Differences in Human Service Work," *Human Service Education* 25, no. 1 (2005): 53–63.

policies that interfered with their religious practices and, in many cases, to win.[164]

Although the Religious Freedom Restoration Act has been cited repeatedly in culture war battles, it is an example of political and social groups coming together in the real world to create a win-win situation. Becoming politically knowledgeable and well-versed also includes open-mindedness and good faith participation in the social and political real world so people can learn from those with different views, work in partnership, and humanize them without seeing them as some sort of evil "other." Often, working shoulder to shoulder with someone who holds a different political view will help us realize that we have been hoodwinked by social and mass media.

Conclusion

I began this chapter with a personal story and would like to end it this same way. In November of 2023, I emailed the editor of one of Iowa's largest (per circulation) newspapers and made a pitch to write a monthly column. I shared with the editor[165] that I was concerned about political polarization and what seems like contempt in American political discourse and how, consequently, mental health is plummeting in both Iowa and America in general. I proposed a monthly column that would create better civil discourse and respect in political engagement and sent her two sample writings. I made it very clear that my writing would examine social issues from both political sides so that greater understanding could occur on both sides, and I was focused on underscoring middle-ground solutions and times when Democrats and Republicans worked together. This editor asked if I could send more samples, so I wrote ten more 500- to 700-word essays.

This editor then made a mistake, accidentally sending an email to me that was supposed to go to an internal colleague at the newspaper. In short, this editor shared how there was not enough controversy in

---

164. Kelsey Dallas, "The Law That Changed Religious Freedom Forever," *Deseret News*, Nov 15, 2023, https://www.deseret.com/2023/11/15/23942010/religious-freedom-restoration-act/.

165. I am purposely keeping the editor's name and newspaper confidential.

the essay to merit a monthly column. It was clear that heated debate, fear-mongering, bizarreness, and disrespect toward others is what hooks people—in the spaces of both social and mass media—and my column would not have any of this. I simply wanted to showcase people with different political views getting along and being open-minded. I sent the same proposal, with the twelve sample essays, to a few other media sources, but no one touched them.

Like this newspaper, too many Americans want to be entertained as they seek information and knowledge related to civic events because it's more exciting than having a somber mind inclined toward reflection. But by earnestly applying the media literacy skills found in this chapter, you can truly become better informed in politics and lower your chances of being hoodwinked by the false messages that are so prevalent in our political society.

5
Richard Haass's Ten Habits of Good Citizens

This chapter, the shortest unit in this book, takes up the work of Richard Haass. In many ways, it serves as a book review of Haass's 2023 publication *The Bill of Obligations: The Ten Habits of Good Citizens.* Haass's book provides a broader view of good citizenship that can aid in lowering contention and increasing social and political politeness—another pathway to make good on George Washington's challenge that Americans become better citizens. But before I share Haass's ten habits of good citizens, I want to give voice to what The Church of Jesus Christ of Latter-day Saints has stated about citizenship.

Counsel from Latter-day Saint Leaders and Sources on Citizenship

If you go to the Church's website and look up the word *citizenship*, it states, "Being a good citizen means more than just obeying the laws of the land. It also means being actively involved in making our community the best possible place for all to live. As we become good citizens of our community, we are doing the will of our Heavenly Father in that regard."[166] It also outlines the twelfth article of faith: "We believe in being subject to kings, presidents, rulers, and magistrates, in obeying, honoring, and sustaining the law." Some of the scripture references on this web page include these:

- "Wherefore, be subject to the powers that be, until he reigns whose right it is to reign, and subdues all enemies under his feet" (Doctrine and Covenants 58:22).
- "And behold, I tell you these things that ye may learn wisdom; that ye may learn that when ye are in the service of your fellow beings ye are only in the service of your God" (Mosiah 2:17)
- "Therefore all things whatsoever ye would that men should do to you, do ye even so to them: for this is the law and the prophets" (Matthew 7:12).

This web page also suggests reading Alma 46 and Doctrine and Covenants 134.

Haass's Bill of Obligations and Ten Habits of Good Citizens[167]

Richard Haass, a veteran diplomat and respected international relations scholar, is president emeritus of the Council on Foreign Relations after serving as its president for twenty years. He served in the Pentagon, State Department, and White House under four presidents, both Democrat and Republican alike, and he is known to have been a close advisor to Secretary of State Colin Powell in the George W. Bush administration. He is the recipient of the Presidential Citizens Medal, which is the State Department's distinguished honor award, and the Tipperary International Peace Award.

---

166. "Citizenship," *Family Home Evening Resource Book* (1997), https://www.churchofjesuschrist.org/study/manual/family-home-evening-resource-book/lesson-ideas/citizenship.

167. Unless another footnote reference is identified, all the information below about Haass's ten habits of good citizens comes from Richard Haass, *The Bill of Obligations: The Ten Habits of Good Citizens* (Penguin Press, 2023).

I learned about Haass's book while attending the Iowa Religious Freedom Day summit in 2023, as one of the keynote speakers, Judge Thomas B. Griffith (who wrote the foreword of this book), strongly recommended that the audience read a brand-new book that he just read called *The Bill of Obligations*. So I purchased it and had difficulty putting it down once I began reading. A few of Haass's suggestions, such as his first one, have been given voice in *Cease to Contend,* but I want to share the entire ten obligations that he posits are at the heart of good citizenship because they are outstanding. The principal argument of *The Bill of Obligations* is that American democracy will endure only if obligations join rights at the core of citizenship, and obligations are behaviors that should happen but are not required. These ten habits (or obligations) will also help lower contention and increase social and political civility.

Habit 1: Be Informed

Haass begins by directly quoting Thomas Jefferson that "whenever the people are well informed, they can be trusted with their own government"[168] and then outlines how Barack Obama made a similar point when he stated, "This democracy doesn't work if we don't have an informed citizenry."[169]

To Haass, an informed citizenry is people who understand the fundamentals of how the government, economy, and society operate and have some understanding of the history of the United States. This can include such knowledge as the fundamentals of the Constitution, representative (not direct) democracy, and how Congress works. Haass argues that those who are uninformed are more vulnerable to being misled by falsehoods, and he argues further that social media often presents a biased and narrow view of the axioms of the American government by being too aligned with the views of the social media base

---

168. "Thomas Jefferson to Richard Price," Library of Congress, Jan. 8, 1789, https://www.loc.gov/exhibits/jefferson/60.html.
169. Barack Obama, quoted in Scott McDonald, "Barack Obama Says Issues, Policies, Facts Don't Matter to American Voters Anymore," *Newsweek*, Nov. 20, 2020, https://www.newsweek.com/barack-obama-says-issues-policies-facts-dont-matter-american-voters-anymore-1547602.

audience. Haass also claims that an informed citizenry understands that a fact is an assertion that can be proven via measurement, such as the actual amount of the national debt or how many people died of COVID-19.

Habit 2: Get Involved

Haass delineates that the power base of a representative democracy, such as in the United States, comes from the people who voted for leadership. He pinpoints how the Declaration of Independence makes this explicit and maintains that democracy requires that citizens take an active part in their democracy. He states the most essential action is voting and shares an example that took place in Croydon, New Hampshire, when a handful of people passed an amendment to slash the town's education budget. The majority of Croydon residents were in total shock when they heard the news and then had to create a special voting session to undo the budget-cutting amendment.

Beyond voting, other political participation can include volunteering for a party or candidate, becoming a member of local election boards, being an election poll worker, or becoming involved in a social cause (e.g., Mothers Against Drunk Driving, Humane Society animal adoptions).

Habit 3: Stay Open to Compromise

In the very first sentence of his chapter on being open to compromise, Haass utters that he was unsure when "compromise" became a four-letter word and shares how too many Americans today believe compromise is viewed as a weakness of character, cowardice, or selling out. Haass underscores how compromise was at the heart of the creation of the Constitution and the Bill of Rights and how our Founding Fathers were viewed as having the strength to compromise. Referring to John F. Kennedy, he advocates that compromise is a test of political courage. Then he quotes Henry Clay, the seventh House speaker, who stated, "All legislation, all government, all society is founded upon the principle of mutual concession."[170]

Habit 4: Remain Civil

Civility is essential to democracy. Haass quotes George W. Bush in his first inaugural address: "Civility is not a tactic or a sentiment; it is the determined choice of trust over cynicism, of community over chaos."[171] Civility allows dialogue and relationship, and opponents of one issue can become partners in other matters. Haass posits that civility can be promoted by dealing with political and social arguments on merit, not making things personal, and not making up the motives behind people's arguments (see chapter 2 of this book related to mind reading). Haass points to how social media has contributed to a higher level of vitriol and contends that there is nothing civil about trying to silence those with whom you disagree, including the free press, as such actions are a form of censorship.

Habit 5: Reject Violence

What makes democracy different from authoritarian systems is that democracy offers peaceful channels for individuals and groups to pursue their political aims. Haass calls for lawful and peaceful protests and brings to light leaders of politically focused nonviolent protesters who were deeply revered, such as Mahatma Gandhi and Martin Luther King Jr. He further augments that both Gandhi and King Jr. avoided violence and opted instead for marches, rallies, speeches, boycotts, and even acts of defiance. Still, all were nonviolent and all had an appeal to conscience.

---

170. Henry Clay's nickname was "the great compromiser." To learn more about him and the quotation above, one good secondary source is David S. Heidler and Jeanne T. Heidler, *Henry Clay: The Essential American* (Random House, 2010).
171. George W. Bush, "First Inaugural Address," The American Presidency Project, Jan. 20, 2001, https://www.presidency.ucsb.edu/documents/inaugural-address-52.

Habit 6: Value Norms

Haass differentiates between laws and norms but postulates that both are needed for democracy to thrive. Whereas the former is enforced by the imposition of penalties, the latter refers to the unwritten traditions, rules, customs, codes of conduct, and practices that make society and political engagement livable. Norms are the underlying spirit of rules, such as respect for authority in democracy (e.g., police officers, governors) or sportsmanship during and at the end of sporting events (e.g., opposing teams shaking hands at the end of a game or series).

Haass states that the most basic norm of American democracy is accepting election results. There's nothing in the Constitution about concession speeches or congratulatory phone calls from the defeated candidate to the victor, nor is there a requirement that an outgoing president ride up Pennsylvania Avenue with their successor and attend their swearing in. However, in the United States, this is a norm that legitimizes the election and shows the highest degree of reverence for the democratic process and hearing the voice of the people. It adds to the sacredness of democracy.

Another norm is that elected and senior appointed officials accept the independent role of the media (more mass media than social media). Haass quotes Thomas Jefferson as saying, "Were it left to me to decide whether we should have a government without newspapers or newspapers without a government, I should not hesitate a moment to prefer the latter."[172] Elected officials who answer questions from respected journalists are a form of accountability in a democracy and have a paramount role (e.g., the midday daily press briefing at the White House where there's a question-and-answer session). Haass also articulates that the release of tax returns on the part of a candidate for high office is also a vital social norm, as it helps to know if there are any conflicts of interest.

---

172. Letter from Thomas Jefferson to Edward Carrington, 16 January 1787," Founders Online, accessed Feb. 4, 2025, https://founders.archives.gov/documents/Jefferson/01-11-02-0047.

Habit 7: Promote the Common Good

The common good is housed within a care ethic toward others. Regarding public health, Haass argues that individual rights do not eclipse when the government provides laws to help the masses. He provides a case example of smoking and how it is now illegal to smoke inside, as secondhand smoke can harm and kill others via cancer. The individual right to smoke inside and harm oneself does not extend to harm toward others. Public health for the common good is part of democracy.

Haass cites Justice John Marshall Harlan, a conservative icon who served as an associate justice of the Supreme Court of the United States from 1877 to 1911, who argued, "There is, of course, a sphere within which the individual may assert the supremacy of his own will and rightfully dispute the authority of any human government. . . . But it is equally true that, in every well-ordered society charged with the duty of conserving the safety of its members, the rights of the individual in respect to his liberty may at times, under pressure of great dangers, be subjected to such restraint, to be enforced by reasonable regulations, as the safety of the general public may demand."[173]

Habit 8: Respect Government Services

Haass outlines a contradiction in American history in that there is a strong American tradition of suspicion toward government, yet the Constitution was crafted to replace the ineffective Articles of Confederation. The contradiction is that a stronger government was needed to originate the Constitution and the Bill of Rights. A free

---

173. Justice John Marshall Harlan wrote the majority opinion that upheld a Massachusetts law requiring residents to be vaccinated against smallpox. Primary source: *Jacobson v. Massachusetts*, 197 U.S. 11 (1905), 11. To this end, Kevin Seamus Hasson makes the same argument about how public health measures can eclipse religious freedom laws in his 2005/2012 book *The Right to Be Wrong*. Hasson is the founder of The Becket Fund for Religious Liberty. In 2011, the International Center for Law and Religion Studies and J. Reuben Clark Law School of Brigham Young University presented Hasson with the International Religious Liberty Award in recognition of his outstanding contributions to promoting and preserving religious freedom.

state allows people to control how it is governed; a state where government interference is extremely limited is antidemocratic.[174] Haass highlights that what began as opposition to strong or big government has morphed into outright hostility to the government and rejection of its authority. Today, trust in the government is very low.

Haass summarizes that the government makes mistakes, including very big mistakes, but the reaction to a flawed government should be a better government, not a complete rejection of authority, such as defunding police departments. He asks us to be mindful of the good aspects of government, such as physical security against local criminals or large terrorist states; the construction of roads, airports, and bridges; vital infrastructure such as clean drinking water and regulation of foods; and the creation of licensure boards, such as for medical doctors, lawyers, and mental health counselors.

Habit 9: Support the Teaching of Civics

Simply stated, Haass worries that most Americans do not understand their heritage or history and probably know less than immigrants who have become new citizens. He cites survey research that suggests that many Americans understand little about their political system. He references Ronald Reagan's presidential farewell address, which stated that feeling good about our nation is not good enough and that what America needs is an informed patriotism that teaches our children the fundamentals about America.[175]

Haass encourages that it is vital for Americans to know that the United States was not grounded on a single religion, race, or ethnicity but was founded on a set of ideas. Although those ideas have not always lived up to their expectations (e.g., slavery and women not being able to vote until 1920), the ideas are the bedrock of our nation. Haass advocates that high schools need to teach civics education and underscores that only eight states and the District of Columbia require a

---

174. Annelien de Dijn, *Freedom: An Unruly History* (Harvard University Press, 2020), 1–12.

175. Ronald Reagan, "Farewell Address to the Nation," Ronald Reagan Presidential Library & Museum, Jan. 11, 1989, https://www.reaganlibrary.gov/archives/speech/farewell-address-nation.

full year of high school civics instruction. Haass then suggests what should be taught in civics classes: the basics of the structure of government (e.g., three federal branches, state and local governments) and how the branches of government operate. He further suggests civics education that explains representative versus direct democracy, republics, checks and balances, federalism, parties, impeachment, filibuster, and how the American economy works. He recommends that students read *The Federalist Papers*, pivotal Supreme Court decisions, and major presidential speeches.

HABIT 10: PUT COUNTRY FIRST

This last obligation is patriotism, which puts the country and American democracy before the party and person. It is core to character, which was known as virtue in earlier times. Haass references James Madison, a Founding Father and our fourth president), who said, "To suppose that any form of government will secure liberty or happiness without any virtue in the people, is a chimerical idea."[176] Haass then references George W. Bush: "The public interest depends on private character, on integrity and tolerance toward others and the rule of conscience in our own life."[177] He also references John F. Kennedy's 1956 book *Profiles in Courage*, where this former president provides narratives of eight US Senators who did the unpopular thing by standing up for compromise or principles when doing so put their careers at risk.[178]

Haass then provides more modern-day examples and explains how a "loyal opposition" is needed in a democracy (rooted in policy and principles, not politics) as its primary role is to put country first by holding the party in power accountable and creating compromise

---

176. James Madison, "Judicial Powers of the National Government, [20 June] 1788," Founders Online, https://founders.archives.gov/documents/Madison/01-11-02-0101.

177. George W. Bush, "Second Inaugural Address," The White House Archives, Jan. 20, 2005, https://georgewbush-whitehouse.archives.gov/infocus/bushrecord/documents/Selected_Speeches_George_W_Bush.pdf.

178. John F. Kennedy, *Profiles in Courage: Decisive Moments in the Lives of Celebrated Americans* (Ishi Press , 2015).

(not to block the party in power automatically). Most recently, this idea was captured by Thomas B. Griffith in the *Deseret News* when he self-disclosed that he yearns for the day when moral character counts in our political leaders, stating that the example leaders set is even more important than the policies they pursue.[179]

Conclusion

Finally, in the last part of Haass's book (the appendix), he provides an excellent list of books and online sources on becoming and remaining an informed citizen. Haass argues that the place to start is to read and study the Declaration of Independence, the Articles of Confederation, the Constitution, and *The Federalist Papers*. He identifies free online classes in civics and invites all Americans to take the test questions given to those who want to become American citizens. He lists the best books about American history and advocates reading past presidents' inaugural and farewell addresses and other famous speeches (e.g., the Gettysburg Address). He identifies some of the most important newspapers, magazines, and radio talk shows, along with presidential libraries and historical sites (e.g., Civil War battlefields), and encourages sitting in on committee hearings (like the state legislature) and volunteering in the political process (such as serving on a jury).

By following Haass's ten habits of good citizens, we can increase social and political civility and decrease contention.

---

179. Thomas B. Griffith, "When Did Moral Character Stop Being Vital to Leadership in Our Democracy?," *Deseret News*, Oct. 30, 2024, https://www.deseret.com/opinion/2024/10/30/is-moral-character-vital-to-leadership-in-a-democracy/.

6

Five Cases of Exemplary Leaders Who Ceased to Contend

As shared earlier in this book, the three-step approach to "cease to contend" consists of three behavioral changes:

- Identify your cognitive distortions to increase social and political civility and lower contention
- Develop better listening skills so you can listen to people who have different political views
- Improve media literacy skills to better navigate social and mass media

Cognitive agility, also known as cognitive flexibility or elasticity, is the ability to adapt your thinking and behavior in response to new situations, changing environments, or unplanned events. Stated another way, cognitive agility is the human ability to mentally move back and forth among many possible scenarios and ideas before focusing on and then acting on the most encouraging one.[180] The opposite

---

180. Gabriella Rosen Kellerman and Martin E. P. Seligman, *Tomorrowmind: Thriving at Work with Resilience, Creativity, and Connection—Now and in an Uncertain Future* (Simon Element, 2023), 71–75, 176–78.

is cognitive rigidity. As I have shared in the *Deseret News*,[181] not only does cognitive rigidity harm us, but it also harms others. It can destroy the broader community and is often at the foundation of mental health disorders. Cognitive rigidity creates contention, whereas cognitive agility helps people cease to contend and increases political and social courtesy.

Five Cases of Exemplary Leaders Who Ceased to Contend

As I shared in the introduction, Pahoran is a powerful example of ceasing to contend. He is well-mannered and civil in the face of Moroni's undeserved criticism and continues to hear (listen to) Moroni's voice. He chooses to focus his mind on rejoicing in the greatness of Moroni's heart, not on being mistreated or on Moroni's poor dispositional or character traits. Pahoran demonstrates cognitive agility, and this type of flexibility in thinking (mindset) will help you, the reader, identify and change cognitive distortions, learn to listen to opposing political views, and gain skills in media literacy.

Now, at the conclusion of this book, I want to provide five examples of exemplary leaders who have chosen the pathway of cognitive agility by choosing not to contend and instead displaying civility and openness to different political and social views and ideas.

Example 1: Abraham Lincoln

In an article I wrote in the *Deseret News*, I shared that the secret to Abraham Lincoln's success was his cognitive elasticity. I am going to draw heavily from this *Deseret News* article.[182]

---

181. Rodney Dieser, "Perspective: Cognitive Rigidity Is Not an American Tradition Why Do We Act Like It Is?," *Deseret News*, Dec. 9, 2022, https://www.deseret.com/2022/12/9/23422660/cognitive-rigidity-partisanship-polarization-lincoln/

182. Rodney Dieser, "Perspective: The Secret to Abraham Lincoln's Success," *Deseret News*, July 10, 2023, https://www.deseret.com/2023/7/10/23789759/abraham-lincoln-elasticity-of-spirit-civil-war-polarization/. The primary source of the Lincoln–Stanton relationship is from Doris Kearns Goodwin, *Team of Rivals: The Political Genius of Abraham Lincoln* (Simon & Schuster, 2006).

Underlying Lincoln's achievements and speeches was his ability to be open-minded, to change his thoughts and opinions, and to listen and learn from others, including those who had opposing viewpoints and were cruel to him, which included Edwin M. Stanton. Serving as the nation's secretary of war under Lincoln, Stanton turned a poorly run War Department into a high-functioning cabinet that helped the North win the war. However, Lincoln's attitude toward Stanton is most remarkable.

Lincoln first met Stanton in the summer of 1855, seven years before Stanton would serve as secretary of war, and in short, Stanton treated Lincoln with contempt. This stemmed from a court case in which both men were involved, McCormick v. Manny, which pitted outstanding patent lawyers against each other. Lincoln had been asked by George Harding (representing Manny) to prepare legal briefs, as the trial was to be held in Chicago and Harding wanted a local lawyer who understood Illinois law. When the case was transferred to Cincinnati, Harding removed Lincoln from the case and partnered with the powerful and brilliant Stanton. However, Lincoln was not informed of his removal, continued to work on the case, and traveled to Cincinnati to be part of the Harding team.

After Lincoln and Stanton met, Stanton took Harding aside, reportedly called Lincoln a long-armed ape, and said, "He does not know anything and can do you no good." In those days, traveling lawyers stayed at the same hotel and ate meals together, but Stanton and Harding excluded Lincoln and would not invite him to their table for meals or to chat. But Lincoln's "elasticity of spirits"[183] took over, and he stayed in Cincinnati for the entire week because he wanted to study how a magnificent and nationally known lawyer (Stanton) argued a case. So moved was he by Stanton's work and legal argument

---

183. In August 1864, Abraham Lincoln invited Wisconsin governor Alexander Williams Randal and Judge Joseph Mills to the Soldier's Home for a discussion on emancipation measures. Later, Mills recorded in his diary, "I was astonished at [Lincoln's] elasticity of spirits." Interview with Alexander W. Randall and Joseph T. Mills, Aug. 19, 1864, quoted from the diary of Joseph T. Mills, *Collected Works of Abraham Lincoln, Volume 7 [Nov. 5, 1863–Sept. 12, 1864]*, University of Michigan Library, https://quod.lib.umich.edu/l/lincoln/lincoln7/1:1109?rgn=div1;view=fulltext.

that Lincoln stood in "rapt attention." He later shared with friends Ralph E. Emerson and his wife Adaline Elizabeth Talcott Emerson that he had never witnessed a presentation so brilliant and thoroughly prepared. He determined from the experience that he should study the law better in order to improve his own skills.

Lincoln had the cognitive flexibility to direct his mind to learn from someone who treated him poorly. In today's climate of political divisiveness and conflict, what Lincoln did is practically unimaginable. At their next encounter, six years later, Lincoln would offer Stanton the most powerful cabinet post because he knew he needed Stanton's superb skill set to win the Civil War. They became and remained very close friends and developed a strong working relationship.

Example 2: George Washington

Constitutional historian Akhil Amar has argued that, like Lincoln, George Washington was renowned for his ability to listen to diverse thoughts and change his mind, but most histories overlook this because they are more focused on Washington's action-oriented leadership and military management.[184] The following three quotation points below, drawn from the renowned George Washington biographer Ron Chernow, articulate Washington's cognitive flexibility:

- "Aware of his defective education, he felt secure in having the best minds at his disposal. He excelled as a leader precisely because he was able to choose and orchestrate bright, strong personalities."[185]
- "Washington invited all department heads to submit opinions on matters, . . . producing sharp collisions and intramural rivalries. . . . This method gave the president a full spectrum of opinions, saving his administration from monolithic uniformity."[186]

---

184. Akhil Reed Amar, *The Words That Made Us: America's Constitutional Conversations, 1760–1840* (Basic Books, 2021), 275–326.
185. Ron Chernow, *Washington: A Life* (Penguin Books, 2011), 596.
186. Chernow, *Washington: A Life*, 601.

- "He wanted to sit at leisure and compare conflicting arguments. Through this tolerant attitude, he created a protective canopy under which subordinates could argue freely, but once decisions were made, he wanted the administration to speak with one voice."[187]

Washington was open-minded, was amenable to changing his thoughts and opinions, and took the time to listen and learn from others, including those with opposing viewpoints.

Example 3: Ida B. Wells and Jane Addams[188]

The historical public debate between Jane Addams and Ida B. Wells on the subject of race, which occurred in 1901, can teach us much about cognitive elasticity. What is so remarkable is that after this debate between two women about a highly intense subject matter—Black men being lynched who were inaccurately stereotyped by white people as being violent and hypersexual—Wells and Addams remained lifelong friends. In her autobiography, Wells referred to Addams as "the greatest woman in the United States." These two women, a Black and white woman, could have attacked each other like so many Democratic and Republican government leaders of today, but they didn't. Instead, despite their public debate, they kept working together and had tremendous respect and admiration despite their acute variance of opinion on race and class differences.

Ida Bell Wells was an American investigative journalist, educator, and early leader in the Civil Rights Movement. She was one of the founders of the National Association for the Advancement of Colored People (NAACP), which was formed in 1909. Wells was born into slavery in July of 1862 during the Civil War. In 1878, after her parents died of yellow fever, she raised her brothers and sister and took a job as a teacher. After the lynching of one of her friends, Wells focused her

---

187. Chernow, *Washington: A Life*, 603.

188. The two primary sources of this debate are Jane Addams, "Respect for Law," *New York Independent*, Jan. 3, 1901, and Ida B. Wells, "Lynching and the Excuse for It," *New York Independent*, May 16, 1901. A secondary source that explains this debate is Bettina Aptheker, *Lynching and Rape: An Exchange of Views* (American Institute of Marxist Studies, 1977).

attention on white mob violence. She questioned the mainstream and whitestream reasons that Black men were lynched (e.g., the argument that white men protect their wives and daughters from hypersexualized and violent-oriented Black men) and set out to investigate. Wells shared her findings in pamphlets and columns in newspapers about the lies and myths being told by white people regarding the lynching of innocent Black men. Her depiction of an 1892 lynching enraged locals, who burned her press and drove her from Memphis. Wells moved to Chicago as the threats on her life intensified.

Jane Addams was born in 1860 into a highly affluent family in Cedarville, Illinois. When she was two years old, her mother passed away, but she continued to be raised by a deeply loving father. John Huey Addams was a founding member of the Illinois Republican Party. He served as an Illinois State Senator from 1855 to 1870 and supported his good friend, Abraham Lincoln, in his candidacies for senator (1854) and the presidency (1860). He was known as the wealthiest man in Stephenson County, had a highly successful agricultural business, and was an abolitionist who was believed to have sheltered runaway slaves (as Cedarville was part of the Underground Railroad).

As you may recall from earlier in this book, Jane Addams went on to open Hull House, a settlement house in a poor district in Chicago, and was the first American woman to receive the Nobel Peace Prize in 1931. She served as vice president of the National American Woman Suffrage Association (1911), first vice president of the Playground Association of America (1912), executive member of the National Association for the Advancement of Colored People (1909), and was a founder of the Women's International League of Peace (1919).

In January 1901, Addams wrote an antilynching article in the *New York Independent* where she condemned lynching; underscored its racist, classist, and sexist origins; and took white women to task for their complicity in the lynching of Black men. Four months later, Wells wrote a rebuttal. Although she agreed with much of Addams's thesis, she felt compelled to challenge Addams's "unfortunate presumption" or failure to argue that lynching was often based on complete fabrications of the character of Black men. Wells was concerned that Addams was propagating the myth or stereotype of the hypersexualized and violent Black man. She took this part of Addams's article to task in the public square.

What is remarkable is that Wells involved no ad hominem antagonism in offering a solid and necessary corrective to Addams. Addams likewise admired Wells and took this opportunity to learn from her. The two women continued to collaborate on behalf of civil justice despite their public disagreement. Addams eventually joined Wells to help found the National Association for the Advancement of Colored People. Wells would go to her grave admiring and respecting Addams. Both women demonstrated an ability to listen to opposing viewpoints and then shared not just friendship but a deep appreciation and veneration for one another.

Example 4: Social and Moral Psychologist Jonathan Haidt[189]

Jonathan Haidt is the Thomas Cooley Professor of Ethical Leadership at New York University in the Stern School of Business and is considered by many as one of the top ten most prominent psychologists of our time. Haidt tells of his transformation from liberalism to conservativism—which he calls stepping out of the moral and political matrix—in his 2012 *New York Times* best-selling book *The Righteous Mind*. The first part of his cognitive elasticity happened after he stepped out of his academic field of psychology, began reading from the very different academic field of anthropology (in particular the academic labor of Richard A. Shweder) about the ethic of community, and then lived in India to study this ethic. Haidt shares the following:

---

189. A word of warning: I am sharing an example of a professor who changed his political views from liberalism to conservativism, and I do not want readers to think I'm pushing a pro-conservative agenda. As I have shared in other parts of this book, my voting record has been one of voting for both liberal and conservative political parties. I hope readers can learn about how this political open-mindedness happened to Haidt when he escaped from his partisan mindset. I hope conservatives reading this book can see some of the good from liberalism by also escaping their partisan mindset, and likewise for liberals reading this book.

Liberalism seemed so obviously ethical. Liberals marched for peace, workers' rights, civil rights, and secularism. The Republican Party was (as we saw it) the party of war, big business, racism, and evangelical Christianity. I could not understand how any thinking person would voluntarily embrace the party of evil, and so I and my fellow liberals looked for psychological explanations of conservatism, but not liberalism. We supported liberal policies because we saw the world clearly and wanted to help people, but they supported conservative policies out of pure self-interest (lower my taxes!) or thinly veiled racism (stop funding welfare programs for minorities!). We never considered the possibility that there were alternative moral worlds in which reducing harm (by helping victims) and increasing fairness (by pursuing group-based equality) were not the main goals. And if we could not imagine other moralities, then we could not believe that conservatives were as sincere in their moral beliefs as we were in ours. . . .

When I returned to America [from India], social conservatives no longer seemed so crazy. I could listen to leaders of the "religious right" such as Jerry Falwell and Pat Robertson with a kind of clinical detachment. They want more prayer and spanking in schools, and less sex education and access to abortion? I didn't think those steps would reduce AIDS and teen pregnancy, but I could see why Christian conservatives wanted to "thicken up" the moral climate of schools and discourage the view that children should be as free as possible to act on their desires. Social conservatives think that welfare programs and feminism increase rates of single motherhood and weaken the traditional social structures that compel men to support their own children? Well, now that I was no longer on the defensive, I could see that those arguments made sense, even if there are also many good effects of liberating women from dependence on men.

I had escaped from my prior partisan mindset (reject first, ask rhetorical questions later) and began to think about liberal and conservative policies as manifestations of deeply conflicting but equally heartfelt visions of the good society. It felt good to be released from partisan anger. And once I was no longer angry, I was no longer committed to reaching the conclusion that righteous anger demands: we are right, they are wrong. I was able to explore new moral matrices, each one supported by its own intellectual traditions. It felt like a kind of awakening.[190]

The second turning point in Haidt's life was when he purposely chose to read books on conservatism with a truly open mind.

Example 5: Modern-Day Prophets of God

During a 2007 press conference immediately after Elder Henry B. Eyring was called into the First Presidency, this new Apostle told this story of the harmony-based disagreement he witnessed among the prophets of God in his first meeting with the First Presidency and Quorum of the Twelve Apostles:

> Here are the prophets of God, and they're disagreeing in an openness that I had never seen in business. In business, you're careful when you're with the bosses, you know. Here they were . . . and I watched this process of them disagreeing and I thought, "Good heavens, I thought revelation would come to them all and they'd all see things the same way, in some sort of, you know." It was more open than anything I had ever seen in all the groups I had ever studied in business. I was just dumbfounded.
>
> But then after a while, the conversation cycled around, and they began to agree, and I saw the most incredible thing. Here are these very strong, very bright people all with different opinions. Suddenly the opinions began to just line up and I thought, "I've seen a miracle. I've seen unity come out of this wonderful, open kind of exchange that I'd never seen in all my studies of government or business or anywhere else." And so I thought, "Oh, what a miracle!"[191]

Although I do not doubt that the Spirit of God played a significant role in harmony-based disagreement, this is an example of cognitive flexibility at its highest level.

---

190. Jonathan Haidt, *The Righteous Mind: Why Good People Are Divided by Politics and Religion* (Vintage, 2012), 126–127.

191. Frank Staheli, "Henry B Eyring - Unanimity in LDS Church Councils," Dec. 22, 2013, YouTube, https://youtu.be/_MZvV6GPhgU.

Your Turn

In closing, allow me to repeat the first few sentences of this book:

As members of The Church of Jesus Christ of Latter-day Saints, we are encouraged to engage in the political process in an informed and civil manner, respecting that fellow members of the Church come from various backgrounds and experiences and have differences of opinion in partisan political matters. We are also encouraged to be responsible, and part of that obligation is to become knowledgeable and well-versed about social, civic, and political issues and events.

We have been commanded to cease to contend. Can we become what George Washington asked of us—better citizens? I have no doubt you can do this, and my humble hope is that this book will help you in this process. Democracy is sacred, and we owe this to our nation.

About the Author

RODNEY B. DIESER PH.D., LMHC IS THE AUTHOR OF SEVEN BOOKS and over 150 academic articles on the topic of mental health and the history of community service. He has written guest opinions for the *Deseret News*, *Chicago Tribune*, and *USA Today*. His writings have appeared in top-notch scholarly periodicals, such as the *History of Psychiatry*, *Journal of Humanistic Counseling*, *Lancet Psychiatry*, *Leisure Science*, and *Mayo Clinic Proceedings*. His most recent historical souvenir book on Frank Lloyd Wright's Walter House in Cedar Rock (Iowa) was the recipient of a 2024 Loren Horton Community History Award by the State Historical Society of Iowa and the 2024 Ney C. Landrum Park History Award by the National Association of State Park Directors for original research in a state park. He works as a professor of health, recreation and community services and serves as an affiliated faculty in clinical mental health counseling at the University of Northern Iowa. He works 10 hours a week as a licensed mental health counselor at Wartburg College in Waverly, Iowa.

Rodney served in the Cedar Falls (Iowa) bishopric for nearly nine years, including as bishop from 2007—2012. He then served on the Cedar Rapids Stake High Council for six years before being called in

October 2022 to serve as a Church history specialist for the State of Iowa. In this current calling, he interviews released Stake Presidents throughout Iowa (going back to the 1980s) and wrote a historical document of the Cedar Rapids Stake (Iowa), all archived at the Church History Department.